LIVING WITHOUT WALLS

a memoir

Julie O'Neill

ONE WOMAN'S JOURNEY FROM FEAR TO
WONDER IN THE HIGH SIERRAS

Cory O'Neill's nationally acclaimed and award-winning photography of the mountain landscapes described in this memoir can be viewed at:

www.coryjoneillphotography.com

"Summer Delight" by Cory O'Neill.
Dusy Basin, Kings Canyon National Park.

To my two favorite men: my dad, Charles, who quietly exposed me to the beauty of the wilderness, and my husband, Cory, who challenged me to explore it.

Wander here a whole summer, if you can. Thousands of God's wild blessings will search you and soak you as if you were sponge, and the big days will go by uncounted... The time will not be taken from the sum of your life. Instead of shortening, it will indefinitely lengthen it and make you truly immortal. Nevermore will time seem short or long, and cares will never again fall heavily on you, but gently and kindly as gifts from heaven.
~John Muir, *National Parks,* 1901

Contents

Chapter 1: The Honeymoon
Chapter 2: Before and After
Chapter 3: The Call of the Wild
Chapter 4: The Early Years
Chapter 5: Finally!
Chapter 6: The Ocean Bar
Chapter 7: Extreme
Chapter 8: Watchful Eyes
Chapter 9: Routines
Chapter 10: Trees
Chapter 11: Nature's Healing Power
Chapter 12: Setbacks
Chapter 13: The Oasis
Chapter 14: Layover days
Chapter 15: Kick the Digital Fix
Chapter 16: Fully Alive
Chapter 17: An Opportunity To Wonder
Chapter 18: The Courtyard
Chapter 19: Find Out
Chapter 20: The Why
Chapter 21: New Identities
Chapter 22: Learning From Fish

Chapter 23: Perfect Timing Redefined
Chapter 24: Shavasana
Chapter 25: Doubt Defeated
Chapter 26: Our Secret Backpacking Weapon
Chapter 27: Boxing on the Trail
Chapter 28: Trail Friends
Chapter 29: Passing Values to the Next Generation
Chapter 30: Siblings with a Different Tune
Chapter 31: The Last Day
Chapter 32: Perspective from 2 ½ mph
Epilogue
Appendix: Eating in the back-country
Endnotes
Acknowledgements
About the Author

Chapter 1

The Honeymoon

Each day is a journey and the journey itself, home.
~ Matsuo Basho, 1689

⟫⟩ˆ⟨⟪

At 8,500 feet, I kicked off my barely two-week old marriage sliding down a snowy embankment, face down and unconscious.

It was day two of our seven-night trip in the Eagle Cap Wilderness of Eastern Oregon. I had spent at least three miles absorbed with my new reality: I was a wife, a spouse, a part of a duo, no longer answering for just myself. Traveling side by side with my college sweetheart was the beginning of a lifetime of doing this together. In my mind I sounded profoundly older as I tossed around my new name: Mrs. I couldn't have been happier.

And then my world went black.

Cory made a quick grab for me, missing by inches. He was left to helplessly watch his new bride slam into the rocks at the base of the snowfield. He leapt down the slope, racing as fast as he could to my unmoving body where he threw down his pack, grabbed the top edge of mine, and rolled me over. My eyes were rolled back into my head. My mouth gaped, and I choked out small breaths and grunts. My legs and back were rigid and straight. He tried to make sense of this nightmare, his mind racing through his emergency wilderness training.

Mike was over 200 feet away across the ravine when he heard Cory scream, "Julie, Julie, breathe!" He fell to his knees and prayed, begging God for a miracle to spare my life.

Just four minutes earlier, there was no sign I was in trouble. My breathing was labored but strong and my muscles were tense with the excitement of the descent. My backpack was loaded with a week's worth of equipment and food. It pressed on my hips and pulled back on my shoulders, forcing me to turn into the slope and use my foot to dig into the snow-covered mountainside.

The dreamlike sparkles of sunlight on the snow stretched before me like a carpet of diamonds as tiny rocks tumbled ahead and lodged themselves in the gullies below. I could see our trail exit about 100 feet below us, and I knew that the nervousness I felt about traversing a steep, snowy slope would disappear the moment I stood on that narrow ribbon of snow-free earth.

I took a deep breath, inhaling cool, crisp air that tasted of sweet tea on a hot day. As I walked, my mind began to wander, which can happen on a trail with endless miles ahead. I concentrated on the descent as needed.

"Help, I need help! Mike, I need help!" Cory cried as he knelt down and cradled my head.

My body relaxed, my eyes closed, and I gave one long final exhale, before I ceased breathing all together. As Mike ran up the slope toward us, he saw Cory hold my lifeless body and put his cheek close to my face, hoping to feel me breathing. Then he unclipped my pack's hip belt and positioned himself to begin CPR. He checked my neck for a pulse, and when he found one, paused momentarily to consider the safety of beginning artificial breathing.

Then, without so much as a twitch, my mouth suddenly opened and I gasped for breath. Two breaths, then three, filled my lungs. My eyes fluttered, and the veil of black turned white. I opened my eyes to find Cory's face contorted with fear.

"How are you feeling? I mean, are you okay?" Cory tried to steady his voice.

"What do you mean? I feel fine." I said. He helped me to my feet.

My mind felt free, disassociated from my body, like I was floating. I looked up the slope. Voices sounded muted and distant. I felt confused but not exactly sick.

I noticed Mike climbing the last switchback to reach me. "Hey, oh my gosh, Mike! What are you doing out here?"

"Really, you don't remember?"

"Okay, okay, what's the joke here, guys?"

Mike and Cory were notorious for messing with my mind; a prank was not out of the ordinary. College roommates for four years, they could finish each other's sentences. Both in rigorous academic programs, they often chilled out with their guitars in the evenings. If they happened to have the same break in their weekly schedules, they'd meet on a muddy trail to power up local forestry roads and single track on their mountain bikes. More times than I can count, I'd stop in to visit after class to find them laughing together, mud-splattered as they hosed down their bikes.

During a particularly difficult time for Cory and me that nearly broke us up for good, Mike showed up at my doorstep, took me out to coffee, and insisted I tell him my side of the story. Equipped with the full picture, he was able to bridge the gap between us, a gap we were not capable of bridging ourselves. We laughed that Mike was the reason we ever made it to marriage. It was only fitting that he'd be by Cory's side during the most terrifying singular event of his life so far.

Mike said, "Well, we're on your honeymoon hike, you know. We planned this months ago. You really don't remember?" He glanced with a furrowed brow and nervous eyes at Cory. They quickly decided that they needed to get me down to the nearby lake basin to a flat spot and an area that was more populated. Fifteen minutes later, on our way down the slope, I collapsed again. This time, Cory was able to watch what was happening and determined that I was having seizures. This seizure left me far more disoriented. My speech was slurred and the fog that settled over my mind was thicker.

We were eight miles and over 2500 feet of climbing from the nearest trail head, surrounded by the stunning granite ridges of the Eagle Cap Wilderness in Northeastern Oregon. A time before cell phones but they wouldn't have been operable in this remote location anyway. Our hiking group of friends numbered eight, only two of whom had any prior backpacking experience. No one in the group had the medical background sufficient to save the life of someone asphyxiating.

Cory and Mike carried me down the final few hundred feet of trail and placed me in a tent to get me out of the sun. Less than an hour later, a third seizure rendered me unconscious, and the seizures repeated every forty-five minutes. With each convulsion, my body became less and less able to return to normal breathing. My conscious mind was not aware of what was happening, my body did not hurt, my mind was floating somewhere between dream-like and completely asleep.

Lying in the tent, I was unresponsive, but still breathing shallowly. Original plans to let me rest and then hike out were abandoned. For thirty long minutes, Cory and Mike hashed out ideas for a new plan, but none seemed workable. The guys weren't sure how many more seizures I could survive. Desperation set in. They were on the edge of a dark abyss, with few options, and as the darkness grew, it threatened to suck us all into a place void of hope. Every moment that passed pushed us all closer to that edge, farther from the known into the depth of the unknown.

As Cory looked out across the expanse to a trail descending into our base camp, what seemed at first to be a mirage in the distance slowly came into focus. My trail angels arrived in the form of a mule train, kicking up dust as they made their way to the water below.

Cory sprinted toward them, calling out, "We need help! We need help!"

The group of horseback riders got closer, and Cory could hardly believe his eyes, for the group that stood before him were forest service personnel, trained for and paid to assist in emergencies. Light suddenly pierced the darkness.

We were in Oregon's largest wilderness area by far, at 361,446 acres. Just when the situation seemed hopeless, these men and women happened by the exact spot. Clearly my time had not yet come. In all the years and miles that we have hiked since that fateful day, we have never crossed paths with a mule train of forest rangers again.

Luckily, they carried with them the only form of communication that worked in such a remote area: a ham radio. They called out to their station that relayed the emergency message to LifeFlight.

Waiting was excruciating. As they monitored my weakening vital signs, time moved so slowly that Cory began to feel faint himself. He was sick to his stomach, helplessly waiting for my only chance of survival to arrive. Then, with the sounds of the helicopter approaching, the impatient crowd snapped into action and Cory's heart skipped a few beats. Help had arrived.

Paramedics jumped out of the helicopter and ran toward my lifeless form, their hair and scrubs blowing in the wind of the whipping blades. As they yelled to Cory over the deafening noise, who brought them up to speed on my condition, I had a sixth seizure. While they attached wires and probes to me, one looked up at Cory and said, "This cycle she's in is not good. We got here in the nick of time. I'm not sure she could have handled many more of these."

Within five minutes of their arrival they had loaded my body with medicine—stopping the seizure activity—noted that my temperature had soared to 106 degrees, and transferred me into the helicopter.

Suddenly the quiet wilderness returned without any evidence that minutes before a giant machine had pierced the silence, landed, and whisked me away to an unknown fate.

Too shocked to cry, Cory stared up into the night sky in disbelief as the helicopter disappeared into the horizon, with Mike by his side. Would I live or die? Then he and Mike hiked through the dark, moonless night, tripping countless times in their pursuit of the hospital.

The next morning, I awoke slowly. I couldn't connect the dots. Nothing made sense. The first things my eyes were able to focus on were a bedraggled Cory and Mike leaning on the window ledge with stooped, tired shoulders and huge grins. They were a mess. Disheveled hair; caked-on dirt covering their limbs and faces; dried blood everywhere; and puffy, bloodshot eyes.

Thankfully, despite the fact that our backpacking trip was completely erased from my memory, I had no problem identifying them.

"Good morning, Jools. How are you feeling?" Cory asked.

"I feel fine! What's going on? Why are you asking me? What am I doing here? You two look like you need a hospital bed more than I do!"

"Hey, do you remember your name?" to which I promptly rattled off my maiden name, despite being an O'Neill for a little over two weeks.

In classic form, they broke the tension by messing with my already confused mind.

"No, that's not right! You and Mike got married. You don't remember?" Cory asked.

"Really? No way. That couldn't be right! What's going on? Am I really married to Mike?" I glanced first to Cory, then to Mike, then back to Cory.

Even in the fog, I felt the intense connection to Cory. The way he looked at me. The way he wouldn't let go of my gaze. I knew in seconds that they were messing with me, and that I was married to the tall, blond guy who couldn't take his eyes off of me. Their peals of laughter did serve to ease my rising nerves, though. *But what was I doing there?*

And then the story started to unfold.

How my brain had fallen into a seizure cycle, rendering me closer to death with each one, without any explanation as to why. How, without intervention, I most likely would not have pulled out of this cycle and would have eventually succumbed to a seizure's grip, never to wake up again.

How Cory and Mike had hiked all night, falling and tripping and getting scraped up as they raced to the closest trailhead to get a lift by the forestry service personnel to their cars, parked hours away. How they drove the rest of the night and finally arrived at the hospital. How they walked through the doors and were greeted by kind staff who immediately realized why they were there. How Cory's first words were, "Is she okay?" How he and Mike wept when the nurse smiled and said the one word he so desperately hoped he'd hear.

"Yes."

Chapter 2

Before and After

*Life loves to be taken by the lapel and told: "I am with you, kid.
Let's go."*
~ *Maya Angelou*

→⟩⌒⟨←

Raised in the fast-paced, paved world of the suburban
Chicago metropolitan area, trails, quiet, solitude, bright blue
skies, and even watching sunrises was not the obvious choice
for a well-planned weekend or summer vacation. It just
wasn't one of my options. Nice sized yards, setback sidewalks,
and large trees lined our cul-de-sac and convinced the locals
to stay put for their entire lives. Neighbors are to the
Midwesterner what adventure is to the Westerner. Weekends
are full of barbecues and pig roasts.

Don't get me wrong. These are great things, too. The
stuff that community is made of. But a wilderness adventure
is the furthest thing from one's mind. Why leave the city? All
the stores, clinics, people, and entertainment are right where

you need them. Big city dwellers often build adventures out of hunting for a purse to match the outfit that was bagged the weekend before.

I remember a conversation I had with my Spanish grandma on the way to the mall one Saturday afternoon that typified a common perspective of city lovers. As we drove on a curvy road through a small grove of trees that somehow had not succumbed to industrialization, she exclaimed, "Ay mia! No me puedo creerlo! *I can't believe it!*" With a tone rising in frustration, she went on in Spanish how horrific it was to have all these trees present. What a waste of valuable space and how dangerous it was to not have civilized this piece of land. Where I saw a nice break in the endless Chicago sprawl, she saw a missed opportunity that created a danger for the citizens.

I never really fit in with this city mindset. I used to pretend the dark clouds lying low in the horizon were actually mountain tops in the distance. I climbed trees and built forts. I cherished the times we went for hikes in the tiny forests near our home. My Oregon-native dad had exposed me to the grandeur of the mountainous landscape on our frequent visits, which seeded in me a dream to someday live where we vacationed. Oregon was, to me, the land of the free-spirited adventurer who roamed the mountains, valleys, and ocean shores powered by mineral water and sprouted greens. I had all Oregonians elevated on pedestals in my childlike, mind's eye. These mountain dwellers were impressive and mysterious.

Our family's move to Oregon in the early 90s gave me my first real shot at assimilation with the outdoorsy

Northwestern breed of humans that I so admired. I wanted to enjoy day-hiking and low-level adventuring, seeing the mountains in the distance. Backpacking was not even on my radar. Walking on the beach? No problem. Fishing? Check. Canoeing? Sounded perfect. These were the outings I had pictured when I envisioned the Oregonian-in-action I was sure to become.

That was before I met Cory. The new love in my life had a different vision, which included me pushing way beyond a sunny walk on the beach.

Cory often talked about taking me backpacking, defining it not as a hobby but as a lifestyle. He had already exposed me to the formidable sport of mountain biking on trails; now it was time to hike them. So a little more than a year after being together, I was challenged to a bona fide Oregon activity—hit the trail and spend the night. This was Cory's sacred activity and an invitation to join his inner circle. Introducing me to the world of backpacking was on the same level, in Cory's mind, as introducing me to his family.

Saying yes to this invitation was saying yes to letting our relationship go to the next level. We planned the trip for late August, which has the best chance of rain-free weather. I was thoroughly excited with no hint of nervousness. I pictured the days, full of beautiful scenery and easy walking, and thought the trip would be a piece of cake. I had seen plenty of pictures of happy hikers and quickly deduced that I would join the ranks of all the glossy magazine characters who graced the pages of the Eddie Bauer catalog.

My first surprise came when I attempted to lift my borrowed heavy exterior-frame backpack. There was no way I could muscle this behemoth to its resting spot on my body. Thankfully, I would have either Cory or his brother, Tim, to heave this monstrosity onto my weak frame. The next surprise came when I took my first steps. I wobbled precariously with my top-heavy load, trying to keep myself upright, so that I wouldn't completely embarrass myself in front of these two mountain men. It occurred to me at that point that I might be in over my head.

Knowing nothing about life on the trail, I didn't even know what questions were appropriate to ask. But being a long-distance runner and an all-state Illinois athlete gave me a hyper-inflated confidence in my body's ability to handle anything. Besides, one of these brothers was the new love in my life and what can't you do when you are love sick?

So I mustered a smile and set off with Cory and Tim to discover every inch of the 40.7 mile Timberline Trail that circumvents Mt. Hood, just outside of Portland, Oregon. I did not know, however, an important fact when I innocently agreed to this adventure… that the trail has several significant ascents and descents totaling 9,000 feet, mostly at canyon crossings. This was not an easy stroll.

We hit the trail in perfect timing with a massive explosion of wildflowers that graced the slopes under the majestic peak. Gorgeous rivers raced down the sides of the mountain, cascading into waterfalls. During the day, I was in love. I loved the motion and the challenge. I loved the sights, smells, and simplicity. My mind attempted to comprehend the immense beauty of the landscape of Mt. Hood while my body battled saddle sore hips and tired muscles.

I also loved the relaxed, confident, and carefree side of Cory that came out on the trail. Up until this point, I had only seen him in our college setting where he was inundated with homework and tests, standard for a civil engineering student. I fell in love with him even more as I discovered this new rugged, yet tender and sensitive side of him, the liberated guy who lived under the surface of a vigorous course load. I found a guy who came alive setting up camp, and a guy who took the time to notice and stand in awe at a field of flowers or the rising sun.

Despite the fatigued muscles, bruised hips, and elevation changes that were unlike any terrain I had experienced in my flat land running days of Chicago, thankfully, I stayed cheerful and positive. I say thankfully because unbeknownst to me, what seemed like a friendly four-day backpacking trip was actually a "can I really date this girl" test!

Avid backpacker Cory, who often clocked 500-plus trail miles in a summer of hiking, had determined that he could not marry a girl who couldn't athletically and mentally handle the backcountry. He knew himself well enough to know that his marriage would be less fulfilling if he didn't share these special times with his wife. To Cory, the idea of family meant time together, not leaving a wife home for weeks at a time to pursue his own passion. He wanted his wife to feel cherished, not abandoned, so he needed a life-friend who'd hike with him. He didn't care if she cooked well, cleaned the house well, earned a lot of money, or any number of other wifely requirements. He just hoped that the lady he fell in love with also loved to get down and dirty on the trail.

During that first trip there were times of self-doubt as on the most difficult climbs or intimidating evenings I asked myself, *what am I doing out here?* As I experienced the unbelievable darkness of the night and the howl of coyotes, thoughts of bear attacks, cougars, and dangerous people hiding behind bushes swirled through my mind.

I was used to being surrounded by the city, the first ventures into the woods to spend the night unnerved me to the core. My grandma's fears had filtered down to me. I dreaded the nights. Were perpetrators lurking? Were wild animals prowling? After learning that the Northwest was home to actual mountain lions, my attempts to sleep were fitful as I imagined wild cougars or bears charging into my tent. During the day, I feared grave injuries– and the blessed cell phone was not yet mainstream. We were on our own.

Stepping out from under the blanket of protection that I thought the city provided into the woods was no small feat. Maybe I was a better candidate for California beaches, populated resorts, and quaint cafes for my getaways. I should have just pulled out a map and picked my vacation options within the circled areas that included AT&T's coverage range. No wilderness areas need apply.

Luckily, being so enamored with Cory blinded me to these potential fears when asked if I wanted to go, and they didn't surface until I was en route, when turning back was no longer an option. And Cory encouraged me along with a wink and a smile or a kiss at a trail junction.

When we passed other hikers, I often felt like an actress, posing as a backpacker, but really just a city girl in disguise. I felt like a fraud, as if the others were actual hikers and I was just faking my way through. I wondered if they knew that when they passed me. Was I missing some kind of secret gleam that communicated to passers by that I was the real deal? I thought for sure that if stood in a line-up with all these fellow hikers, I could easily be picked out of the crowd as the imposter.

But on the final stretch as the trail ended and gave way to the parking lot at Timberline Lodge, I walked a little taller and realized one thing: pseudo-hiker or not, I had fun. Nothing attacked us. Nothing endangered us. We had just spent four days hiking through fields of flowers, crossing rushing rivers, traversing through pine tree forests, and doing so under the massive peak of Mt. Hood. For four days, I breathed the cleanest air and drank the sweetest water I had ever experienced, under the most vivid blue sky I had ever seen.

Despite the fears that crept in during my first trip, I passed Cory's test with flying colors and a smile on my face. While he sensed my misgivings, he saw that I fought through them, kept it positive, and was physically capable of enjoying the wilderness. With each step forward, uncertainty was replaced with confidence. I could do this! All it took was that one trip to convince me that I, too, loved to backpack. And that was the final sign to Cory that this girl he had nicknamed "Chicago" was outdoorsy enough to be his wife. My love for Cory was the gateway to my love for Creation itself.

Before Mt. Hood, you'd be hard-pressed to find a more unlikely backpacker candidate than me. I had grown up far removed from the Wild West and had no experience in the complicated world of outdoor gear, trip planning, and survival in a wilderness. But soon I was officially hooked on wilderness exploration, and was well on my way to becoming a genuine Northwest backpacking diva, despite my midwest roots.

During those first three years in Oregon I went on two- to three-night backpacking trips whenever possible. I turned into the genuine article I had wondered if I could become. I let go of my fears of the dark woods and a self-confidence emerged, built on the belief that I knew how to do this.

Looking back, I am fascinated at the timing of this new conviction. I had hit my Oregon-wilderness-girl groove on the heels of a catastrophe that had the capacity to shatter my dreams of ever going into the wilderness again.

Some moments divide time. They have the power to split our existence into the before and the after. As the world went dark, and my body careened fast and furiously down that snow field, I was unaware that I had crossed over to the 'after' part of my hiking life.

It seemed quite unlikely that I would ever hike again. From then on with every trail step I lugged, not just a backpack full of gear, but also a mountain of fear that was crippling at times. I felt like an unpredictable time bomb that could detonate at any moment. Obviously, hanging out in isolated, pristine wilderness locations was ludicrous. It was time to hang up the hiking boots and stay closer to home.

Chapter 3

The Call of the Wild

Let children walk with nature...
~ John Muir, 1916 [1]

⇒⸓⸱⇐

Our journey is ever changing, evolving with each person we meet, each corner we turn. We meet people who change our lives. We meet people we never think about again. In that first moment, standing face-to-face, that unknown person straddles both worlds. And as life-changing as meeting one's soulmate is, the moment it happens is often just as ordinary as any other.

I don't even remember the first time Cory and I met, but he recalls that I made a strong impression on him in my short jean shorts. They screamed to him, "This girl is an athlete." Apparently, I didn't stop chatting long enough for him to get a word in and introduce himself, so without the opportunity to at least mention his name or find out mine, I became known to him as "Chicago."

Truth is, I had made a secret resolve to avoid a serious relationship with a man. As a newcomer, I wanted to focus on making friends and getting to know my new home. This chance encounter in a university with over 30,000 students happened on the second day I moved to campus. I didn't realize it then, but my plans to wander freely were already in jeopardy.

At an ice cream social on campus a few weeks later, I looked up from my newly tightly woven coven of female protection to lay my eyes on a potential chink in my anti-men armor. My addition to this group of three girls elevated us to the disturbingly embarrassing, yet slightly flattering name of "The Fab 4." It actually served to create a safe haven that positively told the world I was not available to be singled out. *I come not alone, but as a package of four.* It felt safe. What guy in his right mind would want to break into a wall of estrogen, four females thick?

As I stared at my empty ice cream bowl, my mind high on sugar, I stood to leave the safety of my girl network to grab another scoop of ice cream. Losing my resolve, I whispered to one of the girls, "Who exactly is that tall blond standing by the chocolate ice cream?" to which all three girls responded in chorus, "Oh, that's Cory. He didn't even look at a single girl his entire freshman year. A guy that good looking without a girl on his arm is most definitely, and most obviously, gay."

Gay? Well, that would make staying single easier. With more courage from this new information, I determined that despite being completely filled to overflowing with vanilla ice cream, a little chocolate ice cream might serve me well.

"Hi!" I squeaked, arriving at the buffet of desserts. Why was I so nervous? I had no interest in falling for anyone. It hardly mattered, though, for as I ladled chocolate scoops into my bowl, this man named Cory looked down at me as if I were a fly, irritatingly buzzing around his ear. He barely mumbled a greeting to me before turning to his friend—who I later learned was Mike—and continued on with some joke that left them both laughing as I stood there, painfully aware that I had been officially brushed off.

Weeks later, friends in my house arranged a mystery date for me. All the girls in my house, if they had loving and kind friends, had also been set up on their own mystery dates. It's an easy way to meet people as it's done in the safety of a group. In this case, at least twenty girls in my house waited anxiously in the living room for their guys to arrive. I almost hoped my date would be Cory, but after such a complete and thorough denial over chocolate ice cream, I also didn't really care if it was him. That is until he walked into the house in bright red corduroy pants, a plaid colorful shirt, and a single yellow rose. The minute I saw him, my knees went weak. Was he here for me or someone else? Despite my resolve to singleness, I suddenly hoped, with everything in me, that he was there for me.

When he walked toward me, arm stretched out to hand me the rose he carried, I deduced that he was indeed there for me. Something made this gay guy who brushes girls off at ice cream socials say yes to a date with me. And something made him do something quite romantic for a nineteen-year-old bachelor... he brought me a rose. And something else made this amazingly good-looking guy wear, of all things, hideous red pants and a plaid shirt to our blind date.

Walking straight toward me, I suddenly felt self-conscious in my tight, black cocktail dress that cut me mid-thigh and singled me out as a foreigner in the casual, Patagonia-wearing land of Oregon. I was in heels, with curled hair and red lipstick, greeting a very colorful date who eagerly, and confidently, handed me a rose. My ship from Chicago had just landed in Oregon and this was my first encounter with a real live Oregon boy. Everything about him seemed different from the guys I knew back home. Most of them seemed shy and slightly shifty. My dates up to this point were so young that they really didn't know who they were and I made them nervous. But this guy was obviously different: the first thing that I noticed was his strong confidence. He walked tall. His eyes met mine. *He must know how good he looks*, I remember thinking. He winked at me.

All night my heart fluttered between swooning and defense. No way was this guy going to sweep me off my feet. I needed to keep my distance until I knew him better and could make a more logical decision. *Stay calm. Breathe deep.* Why was my heart beating so fast? When the conversation among the group switched to biking, the guys took the opportunity to put me in my place about the inferiority of running—my favorite sport. The tide finally turned in my favor, making it easier to keep him at arm's length, because this guy liked to bike and he was obnoxious about it. We had nothing in common! I mean, really. *Look at those pants. I think they are brighter red than they were when the date started. Geez, what time was it? Only five minutes from the last time I checked? Would this night ever end?*

As tides consistently ebb and flow, so did the night. Once the group began to split off, I sighed in relief. I had made it to the end and could finally bid my sarcastic date goodnight. But my knight in red pants and plaid shirt had other plans. "Wanna go up to Mary's Peak and walk around?"

I hesitated at first, but then caught a sincerity in his eye that made me say, "Sure" before I could rethink my response. After a quick stop to my room to change into warm clothes and comfortable shoes, I hopped into Cory's Jeep and off to Mary's Peak we went. Hiking under the night sky, Cory hit his stride. Stripped of the clutter of groups, small talk, and city lights, he morphed into the down-to-earth, easy to be around, sensitive soul that he really is. I learned that a year earlier he had lived in Germany as an exchange student, where styles, such as red pants, were the rage. That he had traveled in the Alps and all over Germany, learned ballroom dancing and wind surfed on the Baltic Sea, played soccer at the amazing European level of play, and most importantly, had been able to skip out on the immaturity that plagued American high school seniors. Silently I added classy, mature, and cultured to my growing list of attributes that was quickly tipping the scale back to a new level of enjoyment of this Oregon enigma. He could mountain bike during the day and fox trot at night.

With the sun down, I no longer had to look at his bright red pants and could, instead, just listen to him tell stories that quickly turned to his real passion... a place in Southern California called the Sierra Mountains. He talked of a camp that quietly turned boys' lives around during the two weeks they spent away from their Los Angeles habitats with guides like Cory, backpacking in the heart of the Sierras.

As stories unfolded of the powerful changes that happen when a hurting boy intersects with an untarnished wilderness, the depth of character of the storyteller himself took my breath away. There was no stopping this knight from breaking through. Once the initial walls around my heart crashed down, we continued sharing and laughing as we headed back to his place. We sat in his room lost to time, talking the night away, pausing our conversation only when we noticed the first light from the morning sunrise.

"Can I make you French toast?" Cory asked, with a sweet gleam in his eye.

Over that breakfast I realized that from the beginning of the date—over fifteen hours earlier when I couldn't wait for it to end—to this most enchanting breakfast, my heart had made a 180 degree turn. Over syrup and fried toast, I knew that I had met my soulmate. And if I could have read his mind, I would have seen that he had realized the same thing about a girl who had been known to him for a month only as Chicago and would be his wife in a little less than three years.

After the wedding bells quit ringing, nearly five years passed of us coming and going when we wanted as we lived the easy high life of double incomes and no kids. One warm April day, I slipped into the bathroom to take a home pregnancy test. The ten-minute wait was excruciating. When the results finally appeared, I stared at the little white stick in excited disbelief. My heart began beating wildly in my chest. We were ready to start our family, right? I was both thrilled and concerned. Where we ready for this? That plus sign silently screamed that our lives would never be the same. I turned on my heelsand leapt down the stairs of our tiny rented bungalow in the country.

"Cory? Hon?"

"Yeah?" He called back, completely unaware of the life-changing announcement I was about to make. I saw him sitting at our kitchen table, sized for two, and walked toward him. I stood behind him, leaned over slightly, and put my arms around his chest.

I whispered into his ear, "You're gonna be a daddy."

He angled his head up and met my gaze with his, scrunching up his forehead quizzically, "Are you serious?"

I met his question with a huge smile and showed him the convicting evidence that I gripped in my hand.

He pulled me down onto his lap, grinning, and hugged me. "This is amazing! I can't believe we are going to have a baby!" I saw tears well up in his eyes. I knew then that my college sweetheart was going to be an incredible daddy.

As excited as we were, once the shock died down and a few weeks passed, hidden thoughts and concerns crept in. We wondered if our lives would come to a screeching halt, like it seemed to for the many couples we knew who had already started their families. Did that plus sign really mean our years of adventures would be over until the little pea inside of me graduated from high school? And, just a few months from receiving my masters degree in education, with a due date the following January, there would be no point in looking for my first teaching job. From a childless perspective, looking at a future that would be tied down with children was honest angst.

On that snowy January day our son, Cade, arrived, and all thoughts of anything besides the little warm bundle sleeping in the bassinet disappeared. Blurry-eyed mornings, lack of sleep, and nursing around the clock bled our time together into a formless ball. As we shared in the routines of holding, rocking, feeding, and caring for our new son, a love for him filled our hearts in ways we had never known. Suddenly love for hiking and traveling didn't matter anymore. This love was like no other and I was suddenly content to sit and hold my son for hours, never once thinking of or worried that I'd not be able to hike with a baby.

We remained in the fog of our newborn for months. Then, like a bullhorn on the ocean, Cory's suggestion to try a backpacking trip almost knocked me off my rocking chair. "Hey, he's a good napper, he's a happy guy. We should give it a try!" he argued persuasively.

"We're barely sleeping through the night! Are you kidding me? Take a baby on the trail?"

"Oh, it'll be fun. He can sleep in the tent just as well as he can sleep in his crib. We need to get out of our house!" Cory disappeared into the garage to assess our gear.

I didn't have much to lose. All I had to do was pack Cade's clothes and mine and he'd take care of the rest. In between round-the-clock nursings, I managed to gather blankets and clothes and soon enough, we set foot on our first trail as a family.

We hardly slept. A major diaper blowout leaked outside of the Baby Bjorn that snuggly cradled Cade to my chest. At two a.m., when he wailed on cue on the hour, I understood why we did not see other young families attempting such crazy outings. If I'd known that according to the Outdoor Foundation, 3.5 percent of backpackers are between the ages of six and seventeen, I would have wondered how there were even that many kids on the trail as I crawled out of the tent, bleary-eyed and cross-eyed. Of course, under six wasn't even a category. I most definitely wanted to give up. But despite the challenges we kept at it, learning tricks, and in time, reaping the rewards of longer trips.

However, behind the scenes, in the secret places in my heart, it was even harder to hit the trail than the sleepless nights in the tent would suggest. Heading out into the woods without kids had a dark history for me. Because of this, going with our little son, whom I loved more than anything, was more difficult. But not including him was never an option. And not going was never an option, either.

Every trip I took started off with excitement. I seemed to forgive the wilderness for its dual-personality of both freedom and isolation, and I came back summer after summer, focused on the good. But somewhere along the windy path, the alter ego of the massive wilderness landscape would stealthily extend its fingers into my thoughts, silencing my cheerful trail banter. I held onto these fears internally as the ball was rolling; we were backpackers. But what if *it* happened again?

The addition of our daughter, Bekah, to our hiking team added weight to the rolling ball, making it that much more impossible to stop. It's what the O'Neills did. It's what we still do. Neither child has missed a summer on the trail. Neither has their mom.

For the past eleven years, when truly astonished fellow adult hikers seeing us on the trail have asked, "How do you get your kids out here?" I'd ask myself, "How do I get *myself* out here?" This book is inspired from those questions. They have deep implications and far-reaching consequences. Every time we choose to spend a weekend, a week, or a month exploring a wilderness we are choosing to swim upstream, against cultural norms. Because backpacks do not come with extension cords, we intentionally choose to unplug.

Unplug America, Unplug!

It turns out that if you're an American adult, half of you reading this book will have participated in some form of outdoor recreation. This is a good trend. The trouble is, this outdoor recreating upward trend does not appear to be filtering down to our children. The Outdoor Foundation feels that, "an outdoor lifestyle must be reinforced as not just an American value, but also a family value." But too many adults head out alone, leaving their kids at home. On the trail we met young couples, retired couples, solo female hikers, solo male hikers, folks on a break from work, folks without jobs sorting things out, doctors, engineers, teachers, bankers, and college students, but seldom (once actually) did we ever encounter a family.

Sadly, once we cross over into parenthood, we are more likely to choose to stay on the city side of a trail head.

There was a time in recent history when kids ran more freely, feeling cool soil beneath their feet and the wind swirling on their faces on a dusty mountain trail. But every time we hear this question we wonder if we are becoming an indoor people, addicted to our computer monitors while we miss the explosive firework display as the sun dances across the eastern sky. This question points to a phenomenon that in his book, *Last Child in the Woods*, Richard Louv has named "nature deficit disorder," which he defines as "… the human costs of alienation from nature, among them: diminished use of the senses, attention difficulties, and higher rates of physical and emotional illnesses." [2] According to Louv, we're raising the very first generation of Americans to grow up disconnected with nature and that this broken relationship is making kids overweight, depressed, and distracted.

We are combating an alarming phenomenon where youth participation in outdoor activities is on a decline. [3] Forty-five percent of youth ages thirteen to seventeen say they do not participate in outdoor activities simply because they are not interested in the outdoors. Cory and I teach this generation and can attest to this statistic. Whenever we ask our students what they did during the weekend they respond something like this: "Oh I dunno. I slept in, then played video games most of the day."

"Did you fit anything else in?"

"Not really."

If we happened to be talking to athletes, they perhaps broke up the monotony with a soccer or football game, but they still book-ended their game with copious amounts of indoor screen time.

Our American kids like to be plugged in. And I like to be plugged in, too.

But as journalist Jennifer Joy Madden wrote in her *Durable Human Manifesto*, "As much as I like instant access to my loved ones and a world of information at my fingertips, I feel diminished. I worry that we humans have been so bowled over by our Alt-brains of smartphones and Google and GPS, we're developing an inferiority complex. We're disregarding our own amazing powers. No machine can do what [humans] can do" (http://durablehuman.com/).

Because kids are staying inside, they are forgetting how to tap into their own skill set, to create and experience with their full senses, as it's easier to just let a machine do it. Are our modern, techno-kids falling for the lie that they are not amazing, that somehow the machine is superior? Do they go outside, stare at the silence that stares back at them, scratch their heads, and head back inside to see how the Angry Birds are faring?

If we dare to unplug, remove ourselves from our iworld, go outside with our kids and experience life first-hand, children will have no choice but to fall in love with being outside, too. The iworld has successfully duped us all into thinking we are the center of our universe, with information and connections all flowing from each of us. It's a powerful feeling to feel like God. Unplugging, when we are addicted to being in the center of our existence, is intimidating. But doing so, submerging ourselves in an immoveable natural setting, has the powerful effect of reminding us of two basic truths: there is a God and we are not Him. And then, once we wrestle with that for a few trips we move to a deeper reality;

it's nice to let God be God so that we don't have to carry that load. It is then that the deep sigh signals a letting go that opens the gateway for peace, restoration, and the revitalization that is being documented in scientific studies all over the globe. Nature heals.

The Outdoor Foundation points to research, which "dictates that building the critical connection to nature at an early age is vital to the enjoyment of the outdoors later in life... we can all work together to stop America's growing inactivity crisis and repair the disconnect between children and the outdoors." [4] The outdoors sells itself. It's addictive. It's mesmerizing, enchanting. It's exciting and fun.

Modern science is hooking participants up to machines, monitoring their brain waves, and heart conditions. It's taking vials of blood and analyzing them. All in an attempt to document what we all intuitively know, that being outside does something for our souls and bodies. Over 1000 people were studied in some two dozen different forest settings in multiple Japanese studies under the umbrella terms "shinrin-yoku" (which translates as "taking in the forest air" or "forest bathing") and "forest medicine." Sure enough, their fancy devices measured oxygen use in the brain to reveal that twenty minutes of contemplation in a forest setting (vs. urban control) altered cerebral blood flow to a level that is characteristic of a state of relaxation. [5] Spending time walking or contemplating in a forest setting is associated with lower cortisol, lower blood pressure, pulse rate, and increased heart rate variability. [6,7] These lowered stress hormones found in the forest walkers, is proposed to explain the improvement in immune functioning. Compared to time spent in urban built environments, visits to forest settings have been shown to improve natural killer cell activity and the production of anti-cancer proteins. [8]

Inspiration From the Great Men of Wilderness History

Over a century ago, John Muir wrote volumes attempting to convey this same message. He didn't need lab charts to prove what he already knew: nothing compared to being outside.

John Muir has done more to preserve our wilderness than any other American. Prior to Muir, no government in the world had set aside public lands, or recognized them for their own value. His influence on four presidents began with President Benjamin Harrison who preserved thirteen million acres of forest, and continued with President Grover Cleveland who set aside another twenty-one million acres of forests. President William Howard Taft also had a personal tour of Yosemite from Muir.

His greatest influence, though, was on President Theodore Roosevelt (1901-1903). After reading Muir's book *Our National Parks*, he invited himself to go camping in the great Yosemite landscape with Muir, whose wanderings through the wilderness and eloquent writings inspired President Roosevelt to establish 148 million acres of national forest, five national parks, and twenty-three national monuments. Muir's writings spoke of nature as a powerful aid in human health and wholeness for the weary, stressed, and overworked city dweller. It compelled presidents and contemporaries such as Ralph Waldo Emerson to recognize, be inspired by, and spend time in the wild lands of America.

Muir recognized all that could be learned when we are able to run free: "Wildness was ever sounding in our ears, and Nature saw to it that besides school lessons and church lessons some of her own lessons should be learned, perhaps with a view to the time when we should be called to wander in wildness to our heart's content... We... were glorious, we were free—school cares and scoldings, heart thrashings and flesh thrashings alike, were forgotten in the fullness of Nature's glad wildness. These were my first excursions—the beginnings of lifelong wanderings."[9]

Greatly inspired by John Muir's writings of his wanderings, Stephen T. Mather also had a passion for the wilderness. He became the first director of the National Park System in April of 1917, after Woodrow Wilson signed the bill authorizing the establishment of the National Park system on August 25th, 1916. Coincidentally, eighty years later to the day, Cory and I married.

Mather suffered from emotional breakdowns marked by depression and withdrawal. Without drugs to help him cope, he found that spending time, often alone, in the wilderness was his best remedy. When that was not possible, his wife surrounded him in his recovery room with pictures of Yosemite. After months of seclusion, he would emerge, fervently focused on lobbying Congress, the press, businesspeople, and just about everyone in America. His persuasive energetic whirlwind convinced Congress to establish The Grand Canyon National Park in 1919.

Every trip we took did its part to restore us. The challenges paled in comparison to the renewal. Consequently, small trips gave our hiking team the desire for longer and longer trips that took us farther from the trail head each time. Eight years of hiking as a foursome inspired us to dream of tackling a more epic summer. We set our sights on the John Muir Trail (JMT) in California. At over 200 miles, we determined we could physically pull it off when our daughter turned nine. Plans unfolded. We bought our gear and maps. We dreamed. We planned some more. I forced myself to pretend I wasn't scared so plans could progress.

Most of our treks take place on the John Muir Trail. As the premier hiking trail in the United States, it starts in America's treasure, Yosemite National Park, and continues 211 miles through the Ansel Adams Wilderness, Sequoia National Park, King's Canyon National Park, and ends at the highest peak in the continental United States, Mount Whitney at 14,496 ft. It is considered to be the most beautiful thru-hike in America.

In the spirit of John Muir and Stephen T. Mather we hike on as we too have found the power of immersion in nature a powerful way to heal, refocus, calm our spirits, and bond our family together in ways that nothing else can.

Their efforts to preserve public lands make it possible for all of us—in the words of John Muir—to have "places to play in and pray in, where nature may heal and give strength to body and soul alike." [10]

For me, though, the problem was that in nature was where I nearly died. My body and soul needed healing and strength, but the fears that took up residence deep inside me after that day in the Eagle Cap Wilderness nearly suffocated me and my desire to roam free. And I did not, for over a year, even consider doing so again.

Doctors ran full diagnostic tests on me and determined, with their limited understanding, that I am not epileptic. Their explanation—that we all have a threshold, which if crossed, can trigger seizures—seemed more a theory than a fact. A combination of the altitude and low blood sugar flipped a switch in my system. It sounded like this "switch" could flip whenever it wanted to.

My own research has provided more details to this mystery. Seizures are an unspoken side effect of the birth control pill, which I had been taking for exactly one month when the first seizure struck. In fact, epilepsy.com catalogues a plethora of accounts of women who had seizures—usually occurring in the first month after starting this drug. Estrogen triggers seizures. Progesterone is a protector. Estrogen excites brain cells and can make seizures more likely to occur. In contrast, natural progesterone can inhibit or prevent seizures in some women, as it tends to calm those cells down. [11] The pill is linked so closely to seizures that epileptics are cautioned that their anti-seizure drugs reduce the effectiveness of the pill.

The internet, with its limited reach in 1996, yielded no clues of this connection. I read one obscure article a few weeks after I returned home from the hospital that suggested a connection between birth control pills and seizures, but it was not enough to convince me that that was the culprit. I wouldn't connect the birth control pill to these seizures until I was doing research for this very book. So I hiked on for years with this one truth: without warning, I had almost died. Was it the altitude? Was it simply low blood sugar? Was it stress from pulling together a wedding? Was it just faulty wiring (and this was the scariest of all the possibilities)? No real explanation existed in my world at that time. The question plagued me every time I stepped on a trail: is it going to happen again?

Yet somehow, despite these huge fears, the Wild called me to venture back in—or maybe that was just my husband calling, as he couldn't be found anywhere else but in the mountains once July and August arrived. But while his voice was strong, I could have wished him well before he left and greeted him when he returned. Why did I so tenaciously and stubbornly pursue the trail?

Because I had tasted its sweetness. Each time I chose to go, I carried within me a fierce battle between my spirit that found its home, its peace, and its sanctuary in nature, and my flesh that sought to protect my body, whispering to my spirit that freedom was not worth this risk.

Nonetheless, there was a spark within me that continued to yearn for the freedom of the hills. Somehow I knew that if I ever stopped hiking, my quest to break free of the fear that threatened to strangle me would never be overcome.

John Muir's words, spoken as a truth, were not yet my truth: places to play in and pray in… I sensed that the seemingly silent dirt trail beckoning me still had huge lessons to teach me. Maybe if I walked in his very footsteps, along the same trails he walked, I could somehow find myself in a place where nature might heal and give strength to body and soul alike. I would never find out unless I entered in and started walking.

Chapter 4

The Early Years

Quality time is never spent, it is saved and savored.
Remember love is a gift given, not an expectation of return.
The car keys are only sixteen years away; use the time to build trust.
Take him/her mountain climbing early, it builds an inner strength and peace.
Love and forgiveness are opposite sides of the same coin.
Luck, like good times, doesn't just happen, it is created by intention.

~ Advice from Roger Paul , our friend's dad, one month before Cade was born

❧

Through pregnancies, nursing babies, and toddlers, we forged ahead and hiked on. The pull was too strong to choose to stay home. I remember fruitlessly searching for information, tips, and advice, about hauling babies and toddlers out into the wilderness. With little more than a strong desire to at least try, we began to venture in. As it turned out, all we really needed was a desire to go, and the rest figured itself out through trial and error.

Carrying one nursing baby in a front pack and a two-year-old in a Kelty child-carrier backpack, I was fully loaded. Cory had the distinct joy of carrying all the necessary gear. His pack was decidedly too heavy, often weighing in over ninety pounds, but we were at least getting outside, on a trail, and away from the car. The first five years of our children's lives, miles were less of a priority. The focus was to simply enjoy time as a family on the trail.

With our son, we often hiked while he napped in the carrier and stopped to eat and play when he got restless. Quickly we saw that life on the trail mirrored life at home. I had a simple "aha" moment when I realized that naps and mealtimes created the structure for the day in both places. The setting was different, but routines could be maintained as necessary.

And then we had our second.

Number two never slept when we were hiking, nap time or not, as she refused to miss a single thing. She remained wide-eyed and cooing in her backpack perch, taking it all in. With her we learned that she needed a tent to close her eyes. And even then, she often couldn't bear to miss a moment of the action by sleeping.

The process of getting outside with our young kids was laden with piles of gear and needed even more piles of patience. Days were unpredictable; boots might rub little feet wrong, noses could get cold, tummies got hungry, legs were tired, nights could be restless, and of course, it could rain. Packs were full of diapers, wipes, warm clothes, and sippy cups. Some days it all clicked, though; kids hiked well, shoes fit great, sleeping was restful, and the sun shone warmly.

Letting go of expectations was key. Those early year trips were experiments, baby steps to future years where longer trips would be our prize. Juggling all the necessary gear, combined with the constant need for encouragement, cheerleading, close supervision and problem solving explained why more parents chose camping over a hike through Kings Canyon National Park. By putting in the time when our kids were young, we got to experience how absolutely worth doing it really was.

Food and Sleeping

Food weight was less with young children, as nursing and smaller appetites meant that we basically packed for two adults, throwing in a little more for each meal for the kids. Thankfully, by the time their appetites increased to an adult's level, they were carrying their own gear!

Each child adapts to sleeping outside differently. Our son cried throughout the night during one ambitious trip we made with him into the Wallowa Wilderness in Eastern Oregon. At six-months-old, he struggled to reach the hot, cozy temperatures that helped him sleep. I had him dressed in three full body pajamas. We topped him with multiple blankets. My night was restless, of course, as I worried about him smothering in all those layers. When I finally drifted to sleep, he invariably burst into another declaration of revolt.

Lacking sleep quickly robbed the joy from any outing and I began to understand why we seemed alone, with an infant, in the wilderness. It was painfully obvious that most people were simply wiser than the two of us. As the day broke and we puttered around camp, Cade's smiles and giggles returned and we again found purpose in what we were doing. Watching him grab at sticks and rocks as he crawled around camp was the very spark we needed to continue.

What could have been accomplished in a day took us two, but we finally arrived at the beautiful, high mountain Looking Glass Lake. Once there, we stayed for a few days, taking in the scenery and learning to live—outside—with a baby.

Each trip we took presented challenges that required us to work through. For instance, we learned that cloth diapers worked well. We rinsed them with water we hauled from the lake and hung them to dry. The sun disinfected and helped with odors and we didn't have to pack heavy, soiled diapers out with us. Also, in pursuit of a full night sleep, we found that spending a little more money for a thick, winter fleece full body pajama with a hood out performed multiple layers of ordinary "house" pajamas. In fact, clothed in one of these mighty pjs on the trail, Cade often slept better than he did at home. Fresh mountain air and a warm, snuggly pj kept this baby sleeping through the night—even in a tent.

When he returned with us the following summer as a moving one-and-a-half-year-old, we brought a sleeping bag for him that we cut in half and sewed shut, reusing an adult backpacking bag. Still too young to hike, he spent all of the trail miles on my back and truly loved his ride with a view. Pregnant with our second child, I had to fight through morning sickness, but decided I'd rather be sick on the trail than sick and stuck at home. The fresh air and clean water did wonders to energize me, though in fairness to those who have suffered with morning sickness, my case was extremely mild.

The following summer we proactively brought the thick, fleece super pajama for our daughter and bundled and packaged her up for her first night in the tent. When she whined and cried off and on all night, we were perplexed. Years later, we found her in her bedroom with her chest bare, blankets off, and the window cracked open in the dead of winter. This girl liked to sleep cold, so warm and cozy simply kept her irritated and awake.

Unfortunately, there is not a fool-proof manual for hiking with kids. It varies with each family, each child, and each location. My suggestion? Experiment! Start young. Resist leaving the kids at home or not going at all.

Go for it!

Chapter 5

Finally!

This sudden splash into pure wildness - baptism in Nature's warm heart-how utterly happy it made us! Nature streaming into us, wooingly teaching her wonderful glowing lessons, so unlike the dismal grammar ashes and cinders so long thrashed into us. Here without knowing it we still were at school; every wild lesson a love lesson, not whipped but charmed into us.
~ John Muir, 1913 [12]

Day 1: Rush Creek Trailhead to Waugh Lake, June Lake area, California; 8 miles, 3000 ft. elevation change

However you choose to experience nature—with a fishing rod in hand, a gun or bow in tote, aboard a canoe, scaling a rock wall, astride a mountain bike, or with a pack on your back—it can be one of the greatest sources of joy in your life as it connects you to nature the way God intended for us to enjoy it… apart from electronics, machinery, and the man-made gadgets cluttering this planet. Doing so allows the soul and body to heal and be strengthened. It allows God's still and quiet voice to be heard.

And if you have children in your life, bring them along.

For nearly a month, over $1000 of food laid in piles on our kitchen counters and floors, waiting to be packaged, some for the purposes of being shipped ahead in orange Home Depot buckets to drop spots along the trail and some stuffed into our packs for the first leg of the trip. This was just one part of the seemingly endless list that filled our weeks as time marched on toward day one of our John Muir Trail (JMT) adventure.

As much as life stresses and consumes us, it also provides a comfort, a familiarity that I clung to as time ticked on. When the trip was "next summer" it was easy to overlook the challenges that trips like this could include. Visions of hiking along in the warm summer sun prevailed over any negative thoughts that threatened to steal my excitement.

However, on the precipice of our four week, approximately 200-mile backpacking trip that would follow the majority of the JMT, I was surprised at my own feelings. Suddenly I wanted to hold fast to what was comfortable instead of embrace the unknown.

On the night before we left, I had to remind myself that trading in hot showers for cold mountain lake plunges and cushions for tree snags to sit upon was necessary for our family to experience the deep cleanse from toxic city life. As I lay down for the last time on a soft mattress in a climate-controlled trailer, a reality flashed into my mind: we were really going to do this. I needed much more self talk to calm my jittery nerves. My American life is comfortable. To counter this basic truth, I thought back on all the trips we'd taken. No matter how these adventures started, we always hit a glorious groove that trumped all comforts we'd relinquished. That thought ignited a heightened level of anticipation, reminding me of how I felt as a child, trying to sleep on Christmas eve.

We set our alarm for an early departure and eventually drifted to sleep.

The alarm rang at the crack of dawn. We had a lot to do before catching the Yosemite shuttle bus at 8:00 am. We had to finalize packing our backpacks, eat breakfast, take our final showers, tow the trailer north fifteen miles to stow it for the summer, and then drive south to Mammoth Lakes where we'd park our truck and catch the bus.

After months of waiting, it was almost surprising that the waiting was over and it was time to mobilize. Like the first-time dad who knows the time is coming when his wife will actually be in labor but still panics when that time finally arrives, we ran around our camp bumping into each other and sweating more with every passing minute. We darted here and there grabbing items, getting ready, double and triple-checking our packs for gear, and breaking down the trailer for towing.

At one point, we realized we had to go or the bus would leave without us so we threw our packs into the back of the truck with a few other items that still needed to be packed, hooked up the trailer and beelined in the opposite direction of our bus stop to our trailer storage in the quaint town of Lee Vining. As we sat in the truck, en route, I second-guessed our packing and wondered if we'd forgotten someone's backpack in the mayhem. Many a new dad has shown up at the hospital and the carefully pre-planned delivery bag with all of their anticipated needed items is still at home. As I sat in the passenger seat, I became convinced that we either left behind a backpack or we left behind a child.

Hearts racing, we unloaded the trailer; then while Cory and Cade unhitched and stored it, Bekah and I counted. Both kids and all four backpacks? Check. Four pairs of boots? Check. I'd find out later that the only item left behind were my sunglasses.

The kids giggled in nervous excitement as adrenaline surged with the anticipation of the beginning of our trek... and the fact that we were racing against the clock to catch the only bus leaving that day that could take us to our trailhead.

Tires squealed as we turned the last corner to see, to our relief, the bus still at its stop.

"Okay, kids and Mom, I'll drop you off with our packs and you get on the bus. I'll go park the truck and sprint back."

The parking lot was huge, with vehicles staying overnight having to park farther down the mountain, out of the way of the day users. There was a very real chance the bus would leave without Cory.

The scene unfolded in a crazy blur of hiking poles, backpacks, sleeping pads, and food bags being passed in an assembly line fashion from Dad to Bekah to Cade to me to the amused bus driver who helped put the random pile of stuff in the storage compartments below the bus.

"The bus leaves in two minutes," he reminded us.

By now, Bekah and I were chuckling, the tension causing us both to respond with snickers at the craziness before us.

Neither of us mind the spontaneous and unpredictable and secretly thought it would be almost fun to miss the bus. After a stressful morning of trying to gather every detail up in a tight little ball, the irony of spending the day figuring out a creative way to get to the trailhead versus actually hiking on the trail was amusing.

Cade, however, was not amused in the least. A boy who thrives on structure, schedules, and predictability does not find humor in mishaps that could alter plans and set us up for the unknown. So much for looking like pros. There was no way anyone on the bus could have believed that this motley crew of four was about to set sail for a 215-mile backpacking trip. People who do that show up early, with neat packs and tied shoes, and calmly set their intricately packed packs in the storage compartment. They settle down in their chairs with an air of confidence as they quietly gaze out the window lost in thought over the trail miles they have planned for that first day.

We looked like a crazed group who had decided to go for a day hike twenty minutes earlier and grabbed some gear and headed for the bus. As I settled into my seat, the bus doors shut, I looked down the street to see Cory, in full sprint, making his way to his family. He made it to the closed bus doors and knocked. To our relief, the doors opened and we were reunited. We had made it! Before he was even seated, the bus began to pull away from the curb.

The driver must have felt for us as he only charged our entire family six dollars for the hour-long ride. That simple act of kindness was the final encouragement from an outsider that said to me, "You guys can do this. I'm rooting for you!"

An hour later, we unloaded our packs—and the various assortment of gear that had not yet made it into the pack—into a giant pile on the side of the road. We watched our last connection to urban life drive away. Watching the bus turn the final corner, exhilaration surged in our family as there would be no turning back now. We gathered our things and took a few beginning moments' photos.

Even something as monumental as 200 miles on a trail with a nine-year-old-girl and eleven-year-old boy begins at some moment, with a single step. And for us, that moment had finally arrived.

All that was left to do was put on our packs, turn around, and start walking south to our truck parked sixty miles away, as the trail goes, to restock supplies.

Less than a quarter mile into our journey, our cheerful chatter was halted when a man stepped out from behind a bush onto the trail. Angrily, he said, "Do you have a camera or a tripod? If you take any pictures you will be arrested."

After years of dreaming and a year of planning, this was our first greeting. My brain raced for understanding, though the dark-haired, sober-faced security guard stationed a half-mile in from the Rush Creek Trailhead was giving away no clues for clarification. Is there a wanted criminal hiding up the trail? Did we do something wrong? Do we need to turn around?

We came out here to escape the trappings of man, experience freedom. We couldn't fathom what this man meant when he said my photographer husband would be arrested if he took pictures. Did God pull out a copyright license on His creation?

Cory and I let out a few nervous laughs and tried to probe for more information, but the tight-lipped guard held his ground and repeated his warning: "Don't even pull out the camera. It's illegal."

Okay, maybe there's a hidden camera and this is just a joke? This couldn't be right. I literally whipped my head around looking for someone to jump out of a second bush announcing that we were indeed part of a prank. I looked in vain before focusing my attention back on the security guard. He repeated his warning.

A few more nervous banters with the stoic guard revealed the details. "They're filming a movie today. You'll see the set unmistakably up the trail. Absolutely no pictures of the set."

The film was *Oblivion* starring Tom Cruise and Morgan Freeman, and Universal Studios had set up camp, which created a sharp contrast to the natural setting it occupied and the type of camps we like to set up. Over fifty vehicles littered the meadow, though the studio had laid a covering on top of the fragile grasses to minimize the destruction the semi-trucks and motorcoach RVs would wreck on the idyllic setting. From our vantage point nearly 1000 feet above the meadow, we saw little golf carts darting to and fro carrying people to their destinations and a massive white tent that housed the catered meals, a final reminder of the luxuries we were leaving behind as we walked toward a month-long future of sleeping on the ground, sitting on tree stumps, bathing in cold lakes, and eating dehydrated meals.

Such an unusual start to our trip caused trail talk to switch to who these actors were, how much money they made, and what their lives must be like being multi-millionaires. I wondered how many trees we'd have to pass to work this out of our systems. But instead of trees, we passed cable railroad tracks running up the mountain, huge dams, electric wires, massive pipes, and dammed lakes surrounded by stumps. Our quest for natural beauty continued and would not be found in its entirety until the next day.

Walking slowly, we made our way up the steep trail. At first, we felt like rusty machines turning on after lying dormant for a while. Our legs felt unlubed. After the third mile, Bekah slowed down to a painfully sluggish pace. Cade and I naturally pulled ahead, leaving Cory to motivate our youngest up the trail. As we pulled out of earshot, I heard Cory say, "You can do this, Bekah! It's just the first day; take it as slow as you need." Cory had a sweet, quiet, patient spirit, which made him a great "pick up the rear of the caravan" cheerleader. I smiled, knowing she was in good hands and headed up the trail with Cade. I later learned that around mile four, Bekah had casually mentioned, "Daddy? My feet kind of hurt."

"Oh, honey, you're just not used to hiking yet and your feet have to get used to this. It'll be okay. We'll check your shoes at lunch, okay?" he had said.

"Yeah, okay, Daddy."

At lunch, as we settled on our first fallen log to rest in some needed shade, Cory and Bekah talked about her sore feet. "We'll check your shoes after lunch," Cory assured her. But lunch came and went like a long summer sigh and we enjoyed our rest so much that all thoughts of sore feet were forgotten. Taking in the quiet, the birds singing, the river churning, and the blue of the sky, we were completely satisfied, content, and at ease. We ate our last fresh fruit, savoring every last juicy drop of organic peaches, and laughed about nearly missing the bus. We hiked on, not knowing what brewed in Bekah's shoes.

When we showed up to camp at Waugh Lake, the kids pulled out mats and flopped down on the ground. Gently, we prodded them off their mats and let them in on the to-do list. Who was setting up our tent? Cade reluctantly agreed, for it had been nine months since setting up a tent was part of the day's agenda. Quickly, he warmed up to the idea, as with instruction and the space to try, he gained confidence. Like a ball dropping and gaining momentum, he could see the tent take shape and his grumpy reluctance turned to creative energy. "So this pole goes into this slot, right?" In a half hour, the less than ten-minute chore of setting tents up was accomplished.

I settled down on my mat to write in my journal. Just as I finished the first page, my thoughts were interrupted by Cory's concerned voice. "Oh, Bekah," he said, as he squatted down to get a closer look at the backs of her feet, "you have two huge blisters on both heels."

My stomach dropped. Feet health can make or break a trip. My mind flashed back to a notorious trip Cory and his brother Tim had taken as teenagers. Their plan was to hike the entire Oregon section of the Pacific Coast Trail from the California border north to the Washington border. Wearing stout, military sturdy black boots kept their weak soccer strained ankles safe but gave them massive blisters all over the bottom of their feet within the first week of their trek.

Limping off the trail, they gingerly made their way to a nearby road and hitchhiked back to their car, ending their journey 275 miles short of the Oregon/Washington border.

I jumped off my mat and darted straight to our little girl. She sat there calmly, unconcerned, completely unaware of the realities of this new problem. Sure enough, bright red, quarter-sized blisters adorned each ankle.

We kicked ourselves for not noticing the symptoms, but she is not a complainer. Her comments about her feet sounded casual, not alarming. We just stopped and adjusted her shoes but never took her shoes off to double check. As we assessed our situation, we knew that our plans were dependent on our first aid and how quickly Bekah's blisters healed. This was not a good way to kick off a trip where mileage goals must be met each day in order to accomplish the 200 mile trip we had set before us. It was also not a good way to keep things fun for our daughter. We have never been ones to push our kids up the trail. We kept to their pace, their level, and their attention span. If she became miserable, we'd have to make a 180 degree turn and head back to the trailhead and figure out a different way to get to our truck, over sixty miles away.

Lesson #1: Always double-check any foot pain. Do some day hiking, with packs on, in the chosen shoes of the trip to make sure they will work.

The Art of Now

As things wound down that first night, disbelief that our adventure had really started was dotted with apprehension. Bodies were sore, procedures were foggy, one of our teammates had a major setback with blistered feet. The miles ahead seemed both exciting and ominous all at once.

Bekah's double heel blisters forced me to spend much of the night dwelling on the tremendous enterprise for which we had just signed up. Honestly, never once did a moment of doubt cross my mind when we were planning the trip, as we sat at home, snowbound, dreaming of warm summer trail days. But as I sat at camp that first night, and the reality of our endeavor truly sank in for the first time since the conception of the trip, I felt overwhelmed and my confidence wavered. Accomplishing this 200-mile goal required that things went according to plan, every day. And these blisters were not part of the plan.

Having this intrusion on our otherwise exciting first day resonated deep within me. The battle that always raged inside between my athletic-adventurous self and my fearful-what-if-something-goes-wrong self had paused in the excitement of kicking off the trip. If it weren't for the blisters, it might have laid dormant for many days before making its grand appearance back onto center stage in my mind.

Regardless, the battle resurged with power. It was only day one and something major had already emerged. Those cute, youth-sized four, injured feet of our nine-year-old daughter were inadvertently having me confront the ghosts of my past. It wasn't just beautiful landscapes and sunny days out there. People could get hurt, too. My precious kiddos could get hurt. One of them already was.

We took a collective deep breath and went about our evening chores, experiencing for the first time that summer how chilly it becomes when the night descends in the mountains. There were no longer any opportunities to escape to the easy comforts of indoor living. More than once the Hollywood RVs we saw that morning flashed through my mind. I pictured Tom Cruise relaxing on a chaise lounge with a chilled iced tea in hand chatting with Morgan Freeman under the warm glow of a table lamp. They were less than ten miles away, but worlds apart.

Thoughts of the remaining 200 miles swirled with the dark chill of the night, and suddenly, the confident athlete who dreamed up this trip was abandoned and a comfort-seeking, somewhat pouty version of my former self replaced her.

By the time the difficult days came, we would all be trained and able to tackle the them. But we certainly couldn't have done it after this first day. I wanted my super end-of-the-summer power legs without putting in the time it takes to be rewarded with them. I wanted an incident-free summer.

That first night I had to begin to let go. Incidents would come. And each time, so would the wisdom needed to get through it. I needed to believe that. The lessons of the trail got started that first day, not missing a second to begin unraveling my weaknesses and prodding me on to a better version of myself. And I had so much to learn. We all did. Watching my own kids embrace our summer adventure with reckless abandon reminded me of what I once was and what I was hoping to be once again.

It was a good thing we couldn't see into the future, for what awaited us the last weeks of that summer would be the most taxing days in my hiking history. We had eleven passes to climb—each between 11,000 and 12,000 feet in elevation—before we would hang up our packs for the season. And worrying wouldn't add a day to our lives or an ounce of strength to our legs. It was and is a futile waste of time. So why was I so good at it?

Months later, as we sat with a reporter from the *Bend Bulletin* of Bend, Oregon and relayed tales of our summer, our youngest finally had her turn to speak. Her answer to the question of what was her favorite moment of the summer spoke of the natural way that children embrace life—with unbending positive optimism. "My favorite day, it's very different from what everyone else said," she spoke with a giggle as her blond braids bobbed back and forth, "was the first morning. I was so happy because I knew it was the first day, the beginning—and I had the whole trip still left to do." Spoken from the little girl who had developed quarter-sized blisters on both heels that first day.

While I needed self-talk to embrace day one and not become discouraged by the thought of walking over 200 miles, step-by-step over an entire month, our daughter skipped around camp, singing, with blisters on both feet. A shift in thinking from my adult perspective of feeling overwhelmed to a childhood perspective of excitement over all the unknown possibilities that lay ahead could have meant that I spent the morning dancing and singing around camp too.

Instead, the seeds of fear that rooted in me the day my body suddenly collapsed in seizures still festered in the shadows. Honesty hit me with raw reality that what lay ahead were 200 miles of opportunities for me or someone in my family to get hurt or even worse, die.

Bekah was excited by the unknown. I was intimidated by it.

Chapter 6

The Ocean Bar

*Bathed in such beauty, watching the expressions ever varying
on the faces of the mountains, watching the stars, which here
have a glory that the lowlander never dreams of, watching the
circling seasons, listening to the songs of the waters and winds
and birds, would be endless pleasure... One would be at an
endless Godful play, and what speeches and music and acting
and scenery and lights! - sun, moon, stars, auroras. Creation
just beginning, the morning stars "still singing together and all
of the [creatures] of God shouting for joy."*
~ John Muir's journal entry, July 27, 1868 [13]

Day 2: Waugh Lake to camp and a day hike to Donahue
Pass, Yosemite, 5.2 miles

Backpacking with kids guarantees three things:
breathtaking vistas, unbeatable bonding, and a few flying
punches.

In our frequent visits to the Pacific Ocean, I have often marveled at how rough the bar can be on the calmest of days. This is the notorious spot on the ocean where the river pours into the open sea and boats have to deal with this transition area of rough water before they can enjoy the calmer ocean. We were in the bar—relationships, chores, hiking, routines—it was all rough water during those first days. We were experienced but even so, there is always a bar that divides the river from open sailing, and we were not sailing free yet. Waking up at Waugh Lake to kids fighting in their tent, gave Cory and me pause.

Everything I did on that first morning felt awkward. In my warm sleeping bag I realized I needed to use the "ladies room," but I also needed to put on my contacts so I could see past my nose and find warmer clothes to take on the morning nip in the air. I had to figure out which order made the most sense. After my eventual exit from the tent, I walked around in circles for an hour, inefficiently accomplishing tasks. No one knew who was taking tents down or getting water. Cory quietly went about his business and produced some hot water for breakfast. I marveled at how easy he always made it look. Life out in the backcountry is truly second nature to him.

Cade's comment was the most honest of all and was so accurate. Lying awake in the tent thinking about all that he needed to do, his first morning thought, he later admitted, was, "I don't wanna do it!" House routines are easy and mindless—wander down to the bathroom, do your business and emerge with teeth brushed, hair combed, and voilà, you are ready for the day. At camp, every detail took effort, effort we were not used to giving. There was no way to fudge, as we could not leave our beds unmade out there! They came with us everywhere and had to be tidy.

Two hours later, we were still at camp, but the tents were packed (It took Bekah and me three attempts, but then we celebrated with a high-five victory slap) and water was almost pumped.

Happy chirps from Bekah as she tossed rocks with Cade at Waugh Lake's shore told us her blisters were not hurting too bad at that moment. Most likely, the reality was that she was so taken in with her surroundings that she did not have time to care. I gave up my liner socks so she could have two layers of socks and one of my hiking sticks and Daddy covered the pesky wounds with surgical tape and tied her shoes tighter.

Lesson #2: For blister prevention: 1. Wear liner socks! 2. Catch them early.

The soundtrack while in that ocean bar was what settled me and propelled me forward with hope—the lake lapping the shore and the breeze in the trees all had a powerful effect against the edginess of the kids with each other or the hours it took to accomplish breakfast. Those gentle voices from nature seemed to be whispering, "Let it go! You can relax out here. Really! It's going to be okay!"

I did know that something good was happening as Bekah had found her song again. Sadly, the pace of life often robs her of her song. It's an easy thermometer into her heart's happiness levels. When things aren't all up to snuff, she unconsciously stops singing. When her heart is content, the joyful overflow comes out in song.

Despite her setback of two very painful blisters, I do not think she stopped humming and singing all morning. That spoke volumes of the impact getting away to locations of restoration has on people, especially as a family. Even with pain, she sang.

With a casual pace, we hiked toward Yosemite National Park and Donahue pass, stopping halfway up the pass to make camp for the night and eat lunch. Stunning white chiseled peaks surrounded our trail and curved through patches of flowers and tarns of water.

"How are your feet, Boo?" I asked.

"Oh, they're fine, Mama!" she said. That couldn't be right, I thought. Thankfully, the nearly level three-mile day we had did not add a lot of strain to her injured heels.

Our spirits soared as all evidence of urban life disappeared. The sun was warm, the sky was blue, the trail was easy, and the mood was high. Just like a page out of an REI catalog, I mused. And then, Bekah's blisters popped. She is an unusually tough girl, one who never even cried when she got any of her vaccination shots. She has crashed on her bike and popped up, with bloody knees, to announce that she was okay. But when her blisters popped, her cries came strong and hard. They never show this part in an REI catalogue two-page spread.

Plan B needed to be implemented quickly. We might need to turn back after all. Having had a day on the trail, I was okay with that possibility. We were in this together and that mattered more than meeting hiking goals. Thus began her long foot soaks in the healing cool waters of a Sierra mountain stream, alternated with periods of air-drying in the warm sun. In pure Bekah style, all we heard were songs of contentment as she spent hours diligently executing her blister regime. She amused herself with pine cones, sticks, rocks, water, and just looking around while the rest of us set up camp.

After a couple of hours, Bekah decided she could in fact day hike the three miles to Donohue pass so we could touch Yosemite National Park officially. Without a pack on, she hiked as if the Sierra waters had magically healed the massive blisters. It made for a lighthearted, delightful stroll where excitement about our summer plans began to resurge. Maybe this was going to work out just fine, I thought.

We made it to the southern edge of Yosemite. Peeking over Donohue pass, we gazed over the massive forested Lyell Canyon that had apparently suffered from a record-breaking windstorm months earlier. But from our vantage point at 11,056 feet, all we saw was a perfectly intact, lush forest. It gave perspective to the massiveness of the land we were exploring. Standing there, the complete silence was interrupted only by an occasional bird's song and it all brought an undeniable feeling: peace. Naturalist E.O. Wilson asserted that our connection to nature is deeply ingrained in our genes. He gave a name to this cozy feeling we were experiencing—biophilia—which means literally, "love of life or living systems."

This love of life and living systems has been the focus of much research in a growing field of ecopsychology. In his most well-known study, psychologist Roger Ulrich studied patients recuperating from gall bladder surgery at a Pennsylvania hospital in 1984. In comparing patients with rooms that overlooked a brick wall versus those that overlooked a strand of deciduous trees, he noted that the patients with the park-like setting to gaze at had "shorter hospital stays, fewer negative comments in nurses' notes… and they tended to have lower scores for minor post-surgical complications such as persistent headache or nausea requiring medication. Moreover, the wall-view patients required many more injections of potent painkillers."

Like other researchers, Ulrich found that simply viewing pictures of nature could help patients' recovery. In a study at a Swedish hospital, for instance, he found that heart surgery patients in intensive care units who looked at pictures of trees and water had reduced anxiety and need for pain medications. [14]

These obscure studies bring enormous implications. The peace I felt at Donohue Pass was more than just a "cozy" feeling. Proximity to nature really affects our physiology in real, measurable ways. It really does make us happier, more peaceful, clearer minded. It really does detoxify us.

There is much research fueling the findings that nature is restorative. Stephen Kaplan, PhD, and his wife Rachel Kaplan, PhD, are at the forefront of research in what they call "restorative environments." The Kaplans' work in this field began unintentionally in the 1970s when the USDA Forest Service hired them to research the effects of an outdoor challenge program in a wilderness setting in Michigan's Upper Peninsula. That series of investigations led to findings that have influenced a generation of environmental psychologists. "What we found was incredibly impressive," said Kaplan, a professor in the departments of psychology and computer science and engineering at Michigan. "That wilderness became a laboratory for studying nature's effect on people." [15]

The Kaplans and other psychologists are exploring nature's impact on people. The implications of their findings are influencing everything from architectural designs of schools and healthcare facilities to city planners seeking to create buildings and cities that are psychologically healthy. These nature-focused urban designs are being shown to positively affect people's mental functioning, social relationships, and even physical well-being.

And we need all the help we can get. The bad news: today's children seem to be at risk of having a shorter lifespan than their parents. [16] Obesity in children has doubled over the past thirty years, diabetes in children is increasing, asthma has doubled since the 1980s, and mental health issues such as depression, anxiety, and ADHD has increased considerably in recent decades. Much of this is linked to poor diets and lack of physical activity. The CDC reported in 2005 that only 35 percent of high school students met current recommended levels of physical activity. This lack of physical activity has been associated with lower self esteem, high rates of diabetes and asthma, and attention disorders.

So what are kids doing with all their time? They are sitting in front of the screen. And the screen time is killing them slowly. A study of children without an asthmatic type wheeze at the age of three and-a-half followed up with these same kids when they turned eleven and-a-half. The kids who watched more than two hours a day of TV were almost twice as likely to develop asthma as those kids who watched less than two hours a day.

What's the good news? So much of this can be prevented or treated by simply getting outside. Everything from myopia to asthma to chronic pain issues and ADHD have been shown to be impacted positively when the patient gets outside. It wouldn't hurt to get active when outside, but that tends to happen naturally anyway. Just spending time outside tends to increase physical activity. One study showed that for every hour spent outdoors for a group of ten- to twelve-year-olds, their physical activity increased by twenty-seven minutes a week. And even more noteworthy, the prevalence of being overweight in that group dropped from 41 percent to 27 percent. [17]

That exposure to environmental settings could actually help prevent and treat illnesses is the hypothesis discussed in the April 2001 issue of the *American Journal of Preventative Medicine*. "Unfortunately, the idea that exposure to nature can be restorative is almost invisible or nonexistent in health care," says Dr. Howard Frumkin, professor and chairman of the Department of Environmental and Occupational Health in Emory's Rollins School of Public Health. "Our standard clinical paradigm involves medications more than non-medical approaches, treatment more than prevention. But many people are intuitively drawn to this idea. They feel restored and healthier in a beautiful landscape, for example. And on the other side, many environmentalists work to preserve nature for a range of very good environmental reasons, but forget that one of the major benefits may be human health." [18]

Being in the mountains was most definitely like medicine for our souls. Surrounded by color, smells, sounds, and vistas that our minds could process easily served to calm the heart, mind, and body. Everything from the taste of home we got each night from our dehydrated dinners to the easy chatter that weaved our trail and camp times together, slowly worked to unite our family, strengthening us for all that was yet to come. Yes, our very souls were being fed.

Our first twenty-four-hours offered many opportunities to teach and reteach, giving purpose and eventually independence to our daily tasks. Routines were slow now, but in no time, we would have it down—how to setup and tear down the tent, how to get water for dinner, how to clean the dishes, and how to bathe in a stream.

As dinner cooked (sunny day pasta the first night, chicken pasta pesto the second), the kids loudly played Rummy in their tent. Game time seldom happens at home as someone always has something to do. Without distractions, we noticed each other more. Without TV, we created our own entertainment. Rummy one night. Blackjack the next.

Even in rough waters, a deck of cards between siblings is soothing. It's bonding. It's fun.

The night passed quickly with thoughts of Bekah's painful blisters on our minds. Would we have to cut the trip short? How painful would her blisters get? Would her miles be laced with tears of pain?

Normally we could make plans for the next day, but the uneasiness about her heels that we felt as we said goodnight meant that we went to bed without a clue of what the next day would bring. Indeed, the waves in the ocean bar were rocking our boat.

But the glimpses we could see beyond the bar of the open sea beckoned us on.

Chapter 7

Extreme

Innumerable insects begin to dance... every life cell rejoices, the very rocks seem to tingle with life, and God is felt brooding over everything great and small.

~ John Muir, 1894 [19]

Day 3: To Thousand Island Lake; 5 ½ miles, 2500 ft. elevation change

The morning quiet broke as our awestruck girl skipped across the granite slab declaring with all her might, "This is absolutely the most amazing thing I have ever seen!"

Bekah had already put in twenty minutes at her new part-time job I affectionately named: Operation Heal My Blisters. Earnestly soaking her feet in the cold stream reflected her stubborn resolve to keep her family hiking. As a bonus, the discoveries she made as she sat on the banks of the streams completely captivated her. She left her station just long enough to bring the rest of us in on her discovery and then raced back to her post on the stream.

She discovered a tiny whirlpool formed by the river splitting in a unique way, causing half the water to flow below the rocks and half over the top. Like a ride at Disney World, any ant, pinecone, or twig placed upstream gently floated the currents until it hit a water tornado that it couldn't escape as it was sucked down into the downward swirl to disappear forever. The little hole between the rocks created a square foot on the planet that captured our children's full attention for over an hour.

While we could have stayed at this idyllic spot for hours more, after Cory doctored Bekah's heels, we began our gentle morning hike of 3½ miles with a 1000 foot elevation gain to Thousand Island Pass. Depending on how she fared, we'd either stop and camp on this pass or continue on, as originally planned, down to Thousand Island Lake.

As we hiked and passed like-minded sojourners with jolly exchanges of "good morning" and smiles, I thought, *these people don't seem extreme to me!* Sporting various sized packs, tightly laced boots, and eager smiles, everyone shared one thing in common – they embraced nature and found solace in the quiet.

My mind wandered back to work where a co-worker, surrounded by the din of the city, remarked after hearing of our plans to hike the JMT, "Well, you are quite extreme. What's it like to interact with such extreme people all summer?"

By day three an answer to her question slowly began to emerge. Being "extreme" meant that I was fully engaged in every moment. Instead of starting my work day by powering up the computer and waiting for it to warm up, I was fully responsible for and part of my own warm up to the day's work. Each step of the day was powered by me—not a car I sat in. Each sound I heard was not muffled by walls. These were sounds that normally the roar of the city shuts out, but now they are the backdrop to our day. We were as a team, intricately part of making every moment happen.

Extreme meant life was not happening to us anymore. Instead, we were pushing into life, actively engaging in the present. It seemed to me that this was the closest I could get on earth to how God intended for it to be in the first place.

We lunched on the pass where I did a reading of my journal. We sat under Banner peak on a granite island near a reflective lakelet as I read. Of course, it's fun to star in your own story so the family loved it.

Bekah's eyes widened. "Could I write a story like that? How can I write like that?" She immediately pulled out her notebook, which at this point contained more of a bulleted list of the day's events than a narrative story. She began right there starting on day one, writing a story of our trip thus far, asking every minute or so, "Here's what I wrote... Is that okay to write that?" For the rest of the day, whenever there was a down moment, out came her journal. As she tore through pages in her blank journal, filling them with all that bubbled up inside her, thoughts of her blistered feet began to fade.

Her spirits were high so we hiked on to the lake.

Another Lesson Learned

Later that night, as I walked down to Thousand Island Lake from our more remote campsite on the northern edge of the basin, I watched Bekah and her daddy sitting side by side on the lake's edge, quietly talking. They did not notice me and carried on unaffectedly and wholeheartedly. Her pink bonnet danced with the wind in perfect synchronization with her daddy's hat. I couldn't hear their voices, but I teared up as I watched this priceless moment together. Oh, how easy it can be to get caught up with emails and to-do lists and miss times to just sit together, soaking tired feet in the afternoon sun.

But I had blown it, which is why I was walking the shoreline observing the bonding of two souls and not sitting there myself. A half hour earlier I had volunteered to take our Boo down to the lake to soak her feet. Every other time she soaked her feet, she just enjoyed being lakeside, looking around, playing with the water, and having some time alone. So, I grabbed my mat and book and prepared to enjoy some peace and quiet, until she started crying—loudly—because her heels burned in the water. At first, I was sympathetic but when she wouldn't stop, my fears that our trip was in danger (shocking to realize that's what I thought) and my frustrations that I couldn't just relax with her made me miss a chance to guide her through this. Seeing her daddy patiently sitting with her on the lake's edge gave me the full contrast of a different outcome. I silently turned around and made my way back to camp, alone. I admit that I'm still in process and have a lot to learn (and always will).

Amazingly, as I sat back at camp sadly reflecting on my missed chance, Bekah, all smiles, came skipping up the hill proclaiming, "I'm getting so much wisdom from that guy!" Further inquiries revealed that her daddy taught her that her blisters would heal to which she added, "Every time I dip my heels into the cold water, the cells will get tighter to finally make the skin tougher and turn into superskin! I am getting superskin!"

"What are you learning from me?" I asked with apprehension.

"Oh, you're teaching me how to be a mama!"

Precious words from my daughter shook me into reality. I determined to spend the rest of the afternoon with her. We sat side by side on a delightful (giggly so!) grassy ledge that jutted out from a tall granite rock which provided the perfect back support. With our ribbed sleeping mats beneath us, we had discovered a perfectly ergonomic, cushioned, wingback chair at 9,800 feet. For hours we sat in our luxury chairs, writing in our respective journals, interrupted by an occasional check for spelling, an excited updated reading, or more giggles over a funny memory from the trip so far.

Thank goodness kids are forgiving, especially when they are on the receiving end of genuine effort, a simple, "I'm sorry," and love expressed through togetherness.

As Anne of Green Gables pointed out, "Marilla, isn't it nice to think that tomorrow is a new day with no mistakes in it yet?" [20] And isn't it nice to know that kids are quick to embrace the next moment with this very spirit, giving us adults copious amounts of chances to get it right? I love the resilience of kids.

Children are watching us—for better or for worse—and they do what we do. The pride Bekah had in her version of the story of our trip knitted together our time as she studiously wrote everything she experienced and conducted author readings of her work daily from her perch on a granite slab. She took her book project dead serious because she could see that I did.

The easy response to "How are we doing this?" is wrapped up in this simple answer: they've watched us. They've watched us love and do this thing called *wilderness travel* and have discovered for themselves the joy in the adventure of it all.

With life being as it is—four of us going in four different directions—it's becoming clear that "extreme" business is best combated with "extreme" serenity. Our lives on this fast-paced planet are extreme. It's whirring past us at historically record speeds, with more "inputs" than ever before. Leaving the race track for these granite rocks and quiet streams connects us back to a moment in time, not so long ago, when man walked closer to nature.

Yes, extreme times need extreme responses. My coworker was right after all. I am happy to be extreme.

Watchful Eyes

Walk away quietly in any direction and taste the freedom of the mountaineer. Camp out among the grasses and gentians of glacial meadows, in craggy garden nooks full of nature's darlings. Climb the mountains and get their good tidings, Nature's peace will flow into you as sunshine flows into trees. The winds will blow their own freshness into you and the storms their energy, while cares will drop off like autumn leaves. As age comes on, one source of enjoyment after another is closed, but nature's sources never fail.
~ John Muir, 1901 [21]

Day 4: Thousand Island Lake to Granite Lake; 3 miles, 500 ft. elevation change

After four days together, I started to understand why Raymond Duncan said, "A lot of parents pack up their troubles and send them off to summer camp."

Unfortunately, we *were* summer camp... en total—kitchen crew, activities director, and counselor—twenty-four/seven. We had packed up our troubles and sent them to ourselves!

"Hush! You two are always quarrelling. Why can't you agree once in awhile?"

"We do agree, Mama. Cade wants the largest bowl of granola and so do I."

Since I am not fully functioning until well past noon, I had little brilliance to offer to ease the brewing turmoil. I resonated more with Bill Cosby: "Parents are not interested in justice; they are interested in quiet." At 8:00 a.m., quiet sounded heavenly.

I let my ridiculously bright-eyed-in-the-morning husband take charge. Cory gently reminded them that when they feel frustrated, they should still be careful with their tone. His patience is so deep, even during early mornings.

"But, Daddy, when I ask you things over and over again, that's how you sound when you talk to me!"

I looked up from my quiet time with my bowl of granola and smiled, wondering how Cory would get out of this one and once again, thankful that one of us was functioning before 8:00 a.m.—and that that someone was not me.

Cory paused before responding. "Hey, we are all in process over here. It doesn't make it right even if I do it sometimes. I'm still learning and growing, too."

With another reminder of their listening ears and watching eyes, a resolution bubbled up in my heart—a vow to watch my tone, words, and actions closely. With the clutter of life stripped away like it was, behaviors that hung out in the shadows came into focus. When we are around each other at such concentrated levels, kids easily picked up on them—the good ones and the bad ones—and often chose to pocket them as their own.

After breakfast, Cory doctored Bekah's blisters. The soaking/drying routine had successfully started hardening her skin. Once the heels were dry, Cory applied antiseptic cream, a couple of Band-aids, and then first aid tape over the top, since Band-aids do not adhere to the skin. Mole skin is heralded as the perfect remedy for blisters, but our experience found that it sticks to the skin of the blisters. Peeling mole skin off that has adhered to the blisters serves to peel the skin off as well, which intensifies the problem. It also doesn't work well for hot spots that are threatening to turn into blisters.

The cries from yesterday's soak were replaced with smiles as the cream-Band-aid-surgical-tape trio did its magic. The singing from our Boo resumed and led our parade over an adventurous cross-country traverse around the western end of Thousand Island Lake. We traveled under the massive nearly 13,000 foot Banner Peak through green and purple grassy fields, tarns of water surrounded by red and orange Indian Paintbrush. After the route was determined, we headed up the slope, boulder-hopping until we reached the top, letting Cade lead the way to give him experience. Route finding over rock-terraced slopes provides unique opportunities to challenge the kids to stop and determine the safest and most efficient route.

The relentless wind of the last twenty-four hours continued to pummel us, so we took cover behind tall willow bushes on the top of the pass to eat some freeze-dried organic pineapples, Lara bars, and our personal favorite, pistachio nuts. Ferocious appetites were staved off until lunch, so we ventured over the pass and traversed down the backside to the charming, sparkling Garnett Lake, one of my personal favorites.

Without leaving the trail, we'd never have witnessed the quintessential shot that Cory had dreamed of for years. As we descended on the Garnett side, we paused and turned around to see where we had come from (hint: always pause and look around!) and for the first time saw a stair-stepped, granite shallow waterfall, with bright red Paintbrush flowers and plush grasses lining the banks, culminating at the horizon with the massive Banner Peak.

It made me wonder how often in life I get too comfortable on the well-worn route I am on, refusing to try the unknown, venture off the path, and blaze my own trail. Do I allow time in life to pause, look back to where I've come from, and marvel at the view? Turning around and taking in the perfect scene behind us I could almost hear Mother Nature screaming at me that I needed to learn to take time to stop, pause, and celebrate or risk missing the point altogether.

Learning the Art of Relaxation

We set up camp early, right after lunch, and had an intentionally easy afternoon to continue to acclimatize and not overdo it. But after five hours of "hanging at camp," I began to get restless. As fun as it was to relax, I was still too fresh from the city to be able to really do it. After two "easy" days our muscles were not tired, we appeared acclimatized to

10,000 feet, the book I brought was read, and the chores were done.

When it was warm, we were able to sit around for hours, but twenty-four hours of high winds and cold air made sitting around more laborious than relaxing. I needed to hold it together but with dust blowing in the tent (and come to think of it, in my eyes, hair, and teeth too!) and the lack of movement since lunch, I was feeling blown down, cold, and dare I admit... done.

In between walks to the lake to soak my feet and walks back to camp, I made a bit of a scientific observation of my children who were in the same empty agenda, weather-beaten predicament as I was in.

Get this! They were not aware of a predicament at all.

I am fairly sure that, like God, kids don't live inside our time-driven paradigm. They don't have to fight so hard against the pesky, fast-racing forward click of time because they are doing exactly what they would be doing if they had two minutes, twenty minutes, or nine hours (like we had that day). This might explain why getting to school on time is prefaced with many "Hurry ups!" They do what feels right to do each moment, without the burden of what they should be doing.

For Cade, that meant spending half his time carving a miniaturized boat from a willow branch and half his time swinging rocks into the lake with his handmade-by-Papa sling. Bekah chose to spend hours at the lake soaking her feet and creating random works of art with Garnett Lake silt and water and writing the "Story of Her Life on the Trail" into her journal. She had determined she was the author of a new best-selling book starring her beloved family. The following year she actually entered her story, "Me, My Family, and the Sierras"—with detailed illustrations—into a local fourth grade writing contest and came in 4th place in a pool of nearly 200 stories. It was a good story indeed that we were creating, moment by moment on those high Sierra rocks.

When dinner time rolled around I was excited for two reasons: A) We were starving and shepherd's pie full of an organic veggie blend of potatoes, sweet potatoes, corn, carrots, green beans in a creamy seasoned tofu sauce sounded unfathomable to our continuingly famished family, and B) There was something to do! Sadly, eating something that good—when starving—doesn't actually take up much time as we quickly devoured our meal, promptly ending that entertaining diversion.

Cheers were loud as we ate our rehydrated meal. "On a scale of one being horrid and ten being the most amazing ever, what would you grade this dinner?" I asked the clan. A resounding score of ten echoed off the mountain walls.

In April, with thoughts of trail days far off, we had loaded leftovers into the dehydrator, and now on the trail in August, each night we ate homemade meals of organic veggies and various meats, rices, or pastas. Eating our own homemade dehydrated dinners fed our tired bodies with packed nutrition and created anticipation over each evening meal. Such a pleasant change from the gas-causing, freeze dried meals we once endured. Check out the appendix at the end of this book for a few of our favorite recipes.

With dinner done, we needed to set up our tents so that they were completely free of any bear attractors (aka debearing the tent), brush our teeth, and then dive for cover from the dust and wind assault into our temporary homes for the night to play blackjack. With real bears looking for food, our goal was to disappear into the environment. All deodorants, toothpaste, and toiletries of any kind were stuffed into bear canisters for the night. The only things allowed in the tent were our bodies, our sleeping bags, and a book or two for entertainment.

Perhaps it was the incessant wind, or the dirt flying into my eyes, or the chill in the air that triggered a challenging memory from our early years of marriage. Sitting on a rocky shore of Emerald Lake in the Trinity Alps Wilderness of Northern California during our second year of holy matrimony, I had one of those classic "just married" relapses in marital confidence. As the sun set, I turned to Cory and asked, "If I had not continued hiking after those seizures, would you have still enjoyed being married to me? 'Cause honestly Cory, it would be highly justified for me to never want to do this again."

"Geez, Julie, of course I would." Though Cory's quick response was what I wanted to hear, I questioned his sincerity.

"But you joke that my collapse so soon into our marriage indicated that I was 'defective goods' and maybe I was still under warranty and you could get a refund."

"I was just kidding about that. You know that. Come on, hun, I love you!"

But I couldn't shake it, at least not right away. We live in a performance-based world that starts with soccer league crazed parents screaming to their six-year-old daughter midgame (this is a verbatim quote), "Dominate! Penetrate!" *Penetrate?*

So in my early years of marriage, I was still battling old childhood patterns. As a kid, I performed a lot. I grew up playing piano on stages all over the country with my violin-playing prodigy of a brother, David Klinkenberg. I worked hard in school, earning good grades. I wasn't the best in any of these fields, but I ran with the lead pack. And doing so pierced my sense of self with a double-edged sword. Ultimately, it served to undermine my confidence that I was accepted for simply being me. But nothing stabbed harder than my experiences as a competitive distance runner during my junior year in high school.

I came out of the womb practically running. Friends in elementary school screamed in school-ground terror when I was "it," because they knew they were going to get tagged fast. Ten years later, as an Illinois All-State returning athlete to the track squad, I was running well, scoring consistently, and on a fast track back to the state finals when my right shin screamed in pain. The week of our indoor track conference meet, everything inside of me froze as my doctor scanned the MRI of my leg and said, "You need to stop running. Your tibia bone either has a hairline fracture or is about to have one. All you can do is rest."

His dry tone did not help my rising angst. *They need me doctor! I can't stop running now!*

Like it happened yesterday, I still remember my conversation the next morning with my coach. She had always been kind and encouraging, leading me to believe that she really cared about me as Julie, not just me as a high-scoring member of her large track program. In an instant, the mirage of our relationship shattered, revealing the true essence of her kindness. With squinted, leering eyes she said to me, "You are running, Julie. Take twelve ibuprofen so you can't feel it. We need your points to win this." And with that, she turned abruptly on her heels and headed back to the other team members as they stretched on the grass.

"But, coach, it could break. Those are tight turns in that indoor track." I called after her with defeated, slumped shoulders and angry tears forming in my eyes.

"We need your points, " was all she said as she continued her clipped walk back to the team.

She later went on to win Illinois coach of the year, while I recovered from a tibial stress fracture that did indeed occur as I ran the tight curves during that conference meet but not before scoring a top finishing place for my team. She got what she wanted. I was just collateral damage.

To add insult to this most painful injury, I officially only lettered three years in high school track. Despite going to every practice injured, recreating the workouts in the deep end of the swimming pool all alone, at the year end awards assembly, my coach never called my name to receive a letter for that season. I was invisible.

Trials from childhood can create a strange kind of haunting in our lives—what Nietzsche called Lebensneid, or "life envy": the certainty that if only something had not happened everything would have been marvelous, happy, and better. All this longing for a different outcome can hover forever in a shadow world around us, taunting us, until we miss the point altogether. The bad and the ugly of life can become the tinder that fuels the fire of Lebensneid, unless we smother the fire with this: we are better because of these things. Stronger. Wiser. Richer.

That missing varsity track letter is the stuff of who I am, separated from what I do. My Illinois coach of the year taught me the ugly truth of competitive large school sports, yes, but inadvertently she gave me the beginnings of independence from performance.

In reality, I earned that letter every bit as much that season as any other season. I worked out in that lonely pool, surrounded by plaques that demanded, "No Running," day after day, week after week. I showed up to most track meets, limping my way to my seat on the bleachers, cheering my teammates on to victory. I earned my sense of who I was apart from what I did on the field. And that was a necessary path for me to have to navigate.

In the end, the missing letter turned out to be my favorite one of all because it represented me, stripped of medals and glory. It represented the determination, blood, sweat, and tears spilled out in the quiet solitude of that oh-so-dull swimming pool. No one cheered me on. No one even watched. No one really cared or noticed. But I did. I spent those months in the pool attempting to peak the steep mountain of personal confidence, without public recognition.

At sixteen, though, I did not bag that peak.

Not surprisingly, a few years later, young and married, these yet-to-be resolved issues reared up again. That mountain peak of self-confidence still needed to be conquered. Who we are is so precariously balanced between our past mixing with our present that when an unresolved wound from the past leaks some poison into our reactions, it can take us by surprise. Wounds like this can silently fester if they are not healed. Healed wounds become scars. They serve as simply a reminder of a past challenge but they no longer have a grip. On the other hand, unhealed wounds still do. There's still puss oozing, poisoning reactions.

Such was the case that afternoon on the shores of Emerald Lake. Performing well flirted with my allusions of acceptance, taunting me with this question, "Will he really want you around if...?" Over the years I sorted, filed, and deleted files in the filing cabinet in my mind labeled: How I receive love and acceptance. More mental-housekeeping was obviously still needed as I defiantly faced off with my young husband, questioning the strength of our bond.

My reasoning went something like this. Hiking was not an option for Cory. He knew he loved me, yet he also needed to "test" me on the trail before committing to me. What was that about? For some reason, the humor of that test suddenly was lost on me. Surely, a bait-and-switch maneuver could have undermined our marriage—he signed up for a hiking wife, tested the goods, and secured a hiking wife. But was his love for me, if hiking was stripped away, as strong?

With these newly formed questions running through my mind, I did what any hot-blooded wife would do, I got snippy. "You know, I'm not so sure. You're saying it wouldn't have mattered if I stopped hiking with you, but you are saying that to me from the comfortable vantage point of actually being out here with me. How do you know that if we were having this conversation in a city somewhere, you wouldn't feel at least a little tinge of resentment that I wanted to vacation with you in cabins on a lake, or tent camping near our car, or on a beach with friends?"

"Hun, I married you, for better or for worse, in sickness and in health, remember? We are so much more than just hiking partners. We are life partners. I wouldn't love you even a speck less if you never stepped on a trail again... although I might have to send you postcards!"

"You're always the charming one, aren't you?" I smiled at him. Part of me believed him, yet a small part of me hid away in a recess of my heart and continued to wonder. Our marriage was young enough to still have that "new car smell," shining and sparkling, speaking of low mileage and still under warranty. Like many new cars fresh from the factory, we were still working out the random manufacturing errors that can plague a new car and I had just possibly realized the blinker wasn't working.

Since that day, we have had two children and sixteen more years of confidence-building commitment that underscores the depth of our connection to be infinitely more binding than whether or not I backpack with my mountain man. Intimacy and trust are built brick by brick, slowly over time, as much by walking step by step up a trail as by whispers exchanged on pillows at night.

Poet and author Linda Ellis built her platform on this very concept, writing that life is what happens in the dash between the dates of our birth and our death. Not to reduce it to a mere line between two numbers, but to instead highlight the truth that the thousands of days that blur together into what comprises our lives consists of the thousands of conversations, hugs, smiles, and intimacies that hide inside that dash. And just to remind each of us to make every moment count, you can purchase your very own "Live the Dash" reminder in keychains, necklaces, posters, bookmarks, and bracelet memorabilia. Glad there are reminders like that because in the daily grind, the beauty of having to make another school lunch, wash the sheets again, or scrub the kitchen floor can lose its "in the dash" quality. Yet, these are the moments that stitch our days together and build our stories.

The compilation of the moments in the dash are what our lives are, what our marriage is. In the best-selling memoir, *Commitment*, Elizabeth Gilbert succinctly summarizes marriage this way: "Marriage is those two thousand indistinguishable conversations, chatted over two thousand indistinguishable breakfasts, where intimacy turns like a slow wheel. How do you measure the worth of becoming that familiar to somebody—so utterly well known and so thoroughly ever-present that you become an almost invisible necessity, like air?"

With another indistinguishable day of our marriage coming to a close, we laid another brick in the fortress of our marriage, another seemingly insignificant moment that helped to disinfect my childhood wounds. In its place is now simply a scar—a visual reminder of the battle, yes, but it no longer hurts or leaks poison into my relationships. Now I run for enjoyment. I play piano for enjoyment. I learn and read and write, for enjoyment. These things are a part of the multicolored person that I am, but they are not me en totale. I like it this way.

Days like that long, windy one at Garnett Lake provided the necessary ebb and flow, the ying and the yang, that brought acute awareness of life's simple joys as we lived in the contrasts. It stirred in us a touch of frustration that paralleled the frustrated tone of the cold and windy mountains.

But we also learned to marvel at the variety of moods that that rugged land had. The wind was a driving force that carried dust but also seemed to animate the land, giving a voice to the mountains as it whipped through trees, swirled up dust devils, and surged through canyons with a loud roar. If we listened closely, we could hear the mountains singing us to sleep that night.

This ferocious wind would do wonders the next day, chasing us out of our campsite in record time to discover what was around the next bend. Maybe tomorrow's hike would smooth out the irritated edginess that had blown in.

Chapter 9

Routines

*Another glorious day, the air as delicious to the lungs as nectar
to the tongue.*
~ *John Muir, 1911* [22]

⤚⟩⌒⟨⤙

Day 5: Garnett Lake to Gladys Lake; 8 miles

After sixteen years of marriage, it occurred to me that
while we both love to travel and explore, Cory and I are very
different travelers. I suppose this is the definition of
incompatible, but somehow for us, it worked.

Let me expound. The summer before we hiked the JMT,
our family spent three weeks in the challenging and
endearing country of Nicaragua. The first half we spent with
friends, on their property, working on projects for the locals
who lived in the jungles behind their home. Our friends took
care of us, provided shelter and food, advice, and
transportation. Easy, predictable, and productive. No
problemo.

But when we took off for our own independent exploration of the country, Cory quickly sank into a quiet, despondent, and somewhat lifeless form. The friendly nature of the social Nicaraguan folk—needing half the personal space most Americans insist upon—crowded into Cory's bubble, which began his slow decline.

The Nicaraguan bus fleet, which consists of multi-colored old American school busses, is where their bubble-free culture is best experienced. So we headed across the country on one of these rickety busses, claiming our seats in American style, believing that sitting in our chosen seat meant it was now a taken seat. Bekah and I sat in one seat while Cade and Cory claimed their own space. With each stop—a generous word as the bus merely slowed down while a man precariously hung out the door, grabbed the hand of the next occupant, and pulled him or her aboard—more people were added, seemingly mocking the "maximum occupancy: 72" sign prominently posted on the wall above the driver's head. Unquestioningly, the bus was maxed to capacity but absolute numbers are simply a theory in Nicaragua, whereas the actual practice is the more the merrier. The aisles were completely packed, a few people were on the roof, and yet, the bus continued to slow down and collect more passengers. Where were these people going to go?

As the flat screen mounted on the front of the bus blared 1980s VH1 videos and the heat topped 99 degrees, a couple of people chose my seat and Cory's—obviously occupied—as their place on the bus. Six foot three Cory did not fit in this small-sized country, in this small bus, and in his small seat.

Yet the lady who chose to sit next to him, holding her three-year-old daughter on her lap, saw it differently. She just nuzzled in closer to Cory to make room for her family, where, in his American mind, there was none to be made. Cade could see he needed to move so he dutifully moved from his spot onto his dad's lap. Cory balanced him on his knee, holding him close as sweat dripped down both of their backs.

When Cory glanced back at me, I caught a look from him that I couldn't quite place. Was it horror? Shocked amusement? Or resignation? I started to giggle as Pat Benatar belted over the five-foot-four crowd that had trapped this crazed, wild, foreigner in a hot and sticky cage.

My confidant back-country traveler was crumbling in the Nicaraguan wilderness. And this was just the first two hours of our trip. "I'm wondering if we should head back to our friends' house. I don't think I can do this!" Cory said when we got off the bus.

"Oh, why? We can do this! This is fun! Let's get some food and make a plan."

As we looked around for eateries, our eyes landed at the same time on a dirty white kiosk with cracked plaster and cobwebs clinging to the walls. A red sign, aged with peeling paint, said *arroz y frijoles* (rice and beans). We were all starving and with no other options obvious in the vicinity, we headed over and ordered. While we ate our child-sized portions (indeed, Nicaragua is full of small people with small appetites), that same expression flashed across Cory's face. He was clearly uncomfortable. Hot and hungry don't mix well.

I had never seen this look on him before and studied him with amusement. "What's wrong?" I asked. Besides the humidity and heat, something else was definitely gnawing at him.

I continued, "I thought you liked adventure! What happened to the guy who loves to see what's around the next bend?"

He picked at his food. "First of all, I'm starving and I'm pretty sure that eating here will mean that by this time tomorrow, at least one of us will be commode-hugging sick. And I am so hot and sticky I can't ever get comfortable."

"Really, you think we'll get sick?" It was fun to not be the worried one for a change.

"Yeah, how could we not? Of course I love to see what's around the next bend, when the next bend is safe and I know I will be able to eat and sleep. I don't really want to explore here, because I don't trust anything! Not sure who we can trust, what we can eat, and where we should sleep. What exactly are we going to do for the next ten days?"

"I'd be happy to just find a little small town and stay for the week. Get to know the locals in that one spot. Find our favorite cafe. Settle in. Become a Nica for a week." While I described my perfect agenda for the ten days we had left in Nicaragua, I saw that expression creep back onto Cory's rosy-cheeked face. As we each ate our cup of rice and beans, his conundrum unfolded: he liked adventures, seeing what lies ahead, and pressing on to discover new things. He wanted to sleep, but never could because he couldn't stop sweating. He wanted to eat, really eat, but couldn't because the portions were micro-sized and he didn't trust that the food wouldn't kill him. Furthermore, my adventure-seeking Westerner couldn't stay busy if we settled down in one quaint little Nicaraguan village while I happily walked the streets and chatted with the locals. All he could do was sit on a bench, sweating and starving, as time stopped. And he had no interest in road tripping across a somewhat dangerous Latin American landscape.

While I took advantage of how close the Nicas quickly got with visitors to their country and started up conversations, he craved his space and nervously looked for his non-existent escape route. He looked like he was in severe pain! While I enjoyed the spontaneous nature of not having a plan, he squirmed in his dirty, blue plastic cafe chair because the next ten days were a complete mystery. Cory is a planner. I am most happy when I make sketchy plans and then let the rest unfold on its own.

Did I mention that I was the one in charge of planning those ten days in Nica? From a 3000-mile vantage point in the states, I gave up trying to figure out where the quaint spots existed and decided our best approach was to figure it out as we went. I am content to wait until I get the right vibe, and once I do, once I like the feel of where I find myself, I like to settle in, find my rut and routine in this new vibey place, become a local (if possible) and make friends.

We sat in that outdoor cafe around an aging plastic table and hit the low point of our trip. The kids just quietly looked on, not sure how to proceed with their fearless leadership wavering like we were. What would we do for ten days in this country if we couldn't road trip but we couldn't stay in one spot?

"I'd be fine if we could just find some air-conditioning!" Cory finally said.

We had one possible option. Our friends gave us a name and a phone number of a lady who ran an orphanage close to our resort (resort by the way, is another loose term, a very loose term). We called Maria and left a message, not holding our breath that it would materialize into anything. To our surprise, a few hours later our phone buzzed. Maria had texted us! The friendly side of Nicaragua flashed across my phone, "I'll send Jose to pick you up in the morning." Just the hope we needed as we swatted at small, bird-sized wasps that flew around our Nicaraguan "resort" room.

"See, Cory! This place is great!" I said to him as we settled into bed with the air-conditioning buzzing happily, lulling our kids to sleep. He mumbled something in response, communicating that he might not have been as convinced as I was. At 2:00 a.m., my hypothesis was confirmed when I awoke suddenly to banging in the bathroom.

"Did I mention I hate cockroaches?" Cory called out in a hushed whisper as he battled a two-inch juicy black, nasty looking cockroach. The charms of Nicaragua were not amusing my rugged mountain man.

The next morning we met Maria and immediately hit it off with her. In short order we moved into our room. Maria explained that a team from a California church was showing up in the morning to install solar panels. We later learned that this same team came without an engineer and had prayed one would intersect their path. They came with workers, solar panels, but no experience in wiring or installing a solar system. Our eyes lit up as solar panels had been Cory's winter project; he'd converted our camp trailer to an off-grid, sun-charged, eco-trailer while the snow collected on the ground. Cory now had a purpose. He not only had solar experience, he had a full-on degree in engineering. The Californian team was thrilled to meet him and quickly made him the leader of the brigade.

Bekah is wired much like I am. She shows up to a completely foreign place and immediately begins to make it her own. Within thirty minutes of setting up camp during a backpacking trip, at only five-years-old, she collected fistfuls of flowers and stuck them in every crevice she could find that surrounded our camp. Bouquets graced the fallen log that bordered our site, they circled her head, and they clung to nearby trees. There was little need to "see what was around the next bend" for Bekah; we had arrived so it was time to make it home. Likewise, upon arriving in our Nicaraguan home for the week, she pulled out a couple of Nicaraguan necklaces that she had acquired and hung them on her bunk bed. She sighed happily at her decorating job that declared the bunk bed hers and said, "Let's go meet the kids!"

When she did meet them, she formed quick bonds of friendship that transcended language barriers. Throughout the week she and the orphaned kids played together cheerfully, as if they understood each other. Kids are marvelous that way. Adults may see barriers to friendship (we can't communicate!) but kids just see other kids.

If anything, this smiling language that kids shared is what saved the day for Cade. He was particularly antsy during that week in the orphanage as he, like his daddy, needed to know the plan. The hot, sweaty days bled together in a rather slow pace for Cade. He makes for a fantastic hiking partner as he loves to—no, he needs to—move, explore, and is lured by the adventure. It is a predictable sport, for the most part, that consists of hiking and then living at camp. Seeing new things keeps Cade's fast-paced mind happy and occupied. So when time virtually stopped, the heat pounded down on us, and all American-made agendas were replaced by the relaxed Nicaraguan ones, Cade wasn't sure what to do with himself.

He tried to help his dad, and at times found something he could do, but usually he walked away dejected, as welding, sawing, and connecting electric wires were not feasible tasks for an eleven-year-old. During one of his dejected walks, an energetic boy ran up to him with a huge grin and a baseball bat and asked him, in Spanish, to come play baseball with the group of kids gathered in the field below. Boys do not need to understand the language to sniff out fun. Instantly, Cade took off after his new Nica friend and spent the afternoon playing baseball and soccer as if he were in his own hometown.

Just like that, the four of us found our vacation habitat. Like always, once my sonar detects the right vibe, I am content to move in, and stay put for awhile. Bekah and I played with kids and worked with the tias (aunts) in the kitchen, Cade sweated with the boys on the soccer and baseball fields (i.e., he was moving, therefore, he was happy), and Cory drew engineering plans, connected wires, and constructed towers to hold solar panels high above the banana trees. Had we made plans from our United States vantage point we would have missed this little paradise. The orphanage was perched on a large lake with rolling green hills that fed a herd of thirty-plus goats. A chicken coop sat next to a large vegetable garden that was surrounded by papaya, banana, and pineapple trees. Their goal was to create a sustainable and self-sufficient campus that provided their meat, eggs, fruit, and vegetables as well as to teach the children marketable skills as they were the little army that managed it all.

Our little corner of Nicaragua felt like home. In those ten days, we developed routines and schedules, a daily sameness that felt good. We walked the same routes from our room to the dining hall, campus school, gardens, chicken coop, papaya grove, and the hammocks that overlooked the lake. The tias showed Bekah and me where the lime trees grew and asked us to pick a couple bucket loads. We gathered nearly fifty each morning to make the lime juice for that day's lunch. We chopped them in half, juiced each one, added water and cups of granulated raw sugar. Some mornings, Bekah and I helped the kids with their chores and then collapsed into fits of laughter as we taught each other a song in each other's language or tried to do a craft together. We swung in the hammocks until the lunch bell rang where we reunited with Cory over an authentic Nicaraguan spread of fresh papaya, bananas, and rice and beans. One dinner of fresh goat meat was served that had been slaughtered that morning. Truly delicious food came from that primitive kitchen where the beans cooked outside over a fire all morning in twenty-five gallon stock pots.

Cory was increasingly more exhausted as he worked with American fervor under the relentless humid heat. He insisted on completing the project before we left (and indeed, he met his lofty goal). Thunderstorms ravaged the area every afternoon, delaying progress with daily blackouts. Eventually, these solar panels would allow for light to continue shining when the blackouts hit.

One particular afternoon he spent over an hour looking for the local Nicaraguan man, Guillermo, the only one who could weld their tower parts together. "Geez, we finally have the parts we need, it's not storming, and we have electricity. Our progress has been painfully slow with all these blackouts and delays in getting these parts! We finally have it all together and our workers are missing! Where are they?" He asked me, frustrated.

"I think I saw Guillermo on a hammock just a few minutes ago. Maybe he's taking a siesta? It is siesta time, after all."

"Siestas at 3:00 when everything is finally aligned? We'll never get this done!" He talked slowly and quietly, having little energy left to be animated in any way.

"Maybe they've figured out how to survive this weather. You're an American work horse but these Nicas are happy to get it done mañana (tomorrow)!" We both turned to head to the outdoor living room, where the hammocks hung from the rafters of a most delightful, open-air veranda. Sure enough, sleeping on the longest hammock was Guillermo, long gone into his blissful siesta. Mañana would always come— so why miss a good nap?

I think in the end, they taught each other a few things. Guillermo saw the driven goal-oriented American work ethic that produced a finished product of working solar panels atop twenty-foot towers in a week's time and Cory saw that it was okay to take a siesta because it all works out in the end.

As challenging as it was for a Clydesdale like Cory to assimilate into a culture where "mañana" drives their agenda, his highly-planned, detail-focused, driven leadership was exactly what pulled our team together on the trails of the American west. In Nicaragua, he looked like a fish, flopping on the shore line, begging for oxygen and slowly dying as he worked for eight to ten hour days in the heat, battling mosquitoes, and lacking resources.

But on the trail, he swam freely in his familiar habitat. He knew what was around the next bend, in theory, because he planned the trip closely. With Google Earth technology, he did fly-bys of every inch of our treks, knew how the sun would rise and set on the surrounding craggy peaks (for photographic opportunities), and what camping conditions we could expect. He knew where his next meal was coming from and that he could trust the water he'd methodically treat from the sparkling clean mountain springs. Despite the hot days, the evenings were always cool, guaranteeing his best sleeping of the year. His good friend Mike (not college-years Mike) teases him every winter when he stumbles upon Cory, yet again, zooming around on Google Earth. "You've studied that spot for so long! Do you know what the mosquito levels are looking like, too?"

He might not know the exact bug counts, but he can tell you about everything else, which is remarkable as he has not even been there yet. I don't love the tedious planning, so while Cory keeps his nose buried in maps, trip reports, and of course, Google Earth all winter, I focus on dehydrating food.

I am a strange mix, craving spontaneous and predictable, which balances Cory's precision for planning. Mid-winter, our conversations about our summer plans usually go something like this:

"We need to sit down and map out our summer," says Cory.

"Now? It's only January!" I usually protest.

"But if we want to pull permits, we need to start planning now!"

"But I want to make plans for what we are doing this weekend. Planning for July now makes it feel like I am wishing my life away."

"Come on. Just give me a few minutes!" Cory starts to pull out a map.

"Okay, fine; is ten minutes enough?" I sit down with great intentions to listen and contribute.

"Sure, I'll take what I can get."

I make it about four and a half minutes before my mind begins to drift to our families' current affairs and somehow he can tell that I have left the room though my body sits by his side, attempting to care. The problem is, I hardly want to know the plans that march around in Cory's mind. I just want to hike when it's time to hike and in January, it is not time to hike.

This not-so-attractive trait of mine during the winter works out great for the summer. And it served me well in Nicaragua. I travel with few expectations and a childlike giddiness when the spontaneous unfolds in front of me. I am okay when things don't work out as planned (because I don't really know the plan). The trail becomes home not when we walk the trails that I have dreamed of walking on all year, but instead, when we hit a groove. Hike, eat, set up camp, rest, and repeat. Routines are comfortable, like a favorite sweater, allowing for spontaneous discoveries within their safe boundaries. So, once the summer hits, I am good, Cory's good, and the kids just follow along.

This quirky craving for routines made it nice for me to see the wake-up-to-trail times tighten up from nearly three hours to an hour and a half. It was a good indicator of teamwork and that individual contributions were improving, that we were all slipping into a routine. We were on vacation, after all, so it wasn't like we were running a military boot camp each morning. However, it was hard to believe how fluid our team became in just four mornings. I felt much more confident on the seventh day than I had just four days earlier.

Each summer I recreate my morning routine, surprisingly, changing it every year. I settled, at that point, on putting on my contacts first, stuffing my sleeping bag and mat into their stuff bags, packing my backpack, and then leaving the tent to brush my teeth. With those initial duties completed, I was ready to eat breakfast and begin waking up.

Some mornings, Cade or Bekah chose to stuff their own bags and their sibling's bag, just to help the family team out. We would emerge to the breakfast rock with only the tents left to tear down ready to devour homemade granola full of nuts and seeds.

Despite the incessant and relentless wind, when the morning came, we all fell in love with Garnett Lake as we cross-country trekked from the western edge to the actual

JMT trail. We walked past flowers, waterfalls, and White Bark Pine that spoke of a Master Gardener. Garnett Lake showcased a sunlight dance on its surface that sparkled like thousands of diamonds glistening in the morning sun. Once we crossed the bridge at the outlet and headed up to the pass on the other side of the lake, the roar of the wind finally gave way to a warm, friendly sun that smiled on us as we climbed through flower-lined trails to the 11,000 foot pass.

Though Garnett Lake always charms, the strong winds blowing were a clear reminder that we were but visitors in a wild land that would do what it does without any care to our comfort. We needed to always be prepared, alert, and remain respectful of these wild places, no matter how charmed we became.

Our tribe marched through the day eager to pitch in, lending a hand whenever they could. Children like to work and help and contribute. This is yet another key way to entice children to get outside. It connects them, like it connects adults, to the basics of survival. They, too, like routines. Maybe they drag their feet at home because they aren't able to connect themselves to the big picture as easily as they can outside. Emptying the dishwasher is such a small part of accomplishing a meal, and that doesn't even explain how the mortgage gets paid!

In contrast, when camping, from the moment the stove was lit until the last dish was cleaned, they were part of the process of meal prep and cooking. They were responsible for setting up the tents and their own bedding. Cade assisted in purifying the water. Bekah often helped massage the bags of rehydrated food, infusing life-giving water back into our meals. Cade often cleaned the evening dishes. Splashing in a nearby stream to clean off the days' trail dust was accomplished each evening without reminders as kids learned quickly that it was a race against the setting sun if one wanted a warm bath.

Bekah marveled every morning at how we were able to carry all that we needed (a tangible amount that she could wrap her mind around) on our backs. Even she, at nine, and Cade, at eleven, knew how to set the tents up, pack and unpack their bags, keep clean, light the stove to boil water; that is… survive.

How could a nine-year-old comprehend all that it takes to have a modern, American house full of stuff? The beauty of when we remove ourselves from all of the clutter of life is the leveling effect it has – where seven-, nine-, and eleven-year-olds can become aware of exactly what is needed to get through each day, happy. It makes sense that within a few days of watching us and being coached through procedures their confidence propelled them to eagerly step up to the plate and work hard, with enthusiasm for each task.

That night, as we sat in the trees near Gladys Lake en route to The Devil's Postpile National Monument, where the first leg of our journey ended, Bekah cheerfully massaged the dinner bags to rehydrate them, while Cade was lakeside with Daddy, getting water.

How I loved seeing all of the things that create our adult world stripped away and replaced with dirt, rocks, trees, warm sun, and lakes that allowed our kids to come to life as they saw how their efforts made a big difference in our daily to-do lists. Their chores were directly linked to our survival, which is empowering to a young child. We've noticed over the years, too, that the confidence and work ethic gained out in the wilderness as we worked through each day as a team transferred to their daily lives at home. Leaders from boy scouts to outdoor camp counselors can attest to the same.

Learning routines that includes the kids not only builds confidence, but also helps develop common sense and a sense of safety. I am not willing to let them go free in the woods without us, but in the safety of our company, they have learned what it takes to do just that. And that feels good when you are nine or eleven.

Some motivators are beyond our control. We had little to do with the record breaking 1½ hour time from wake up to hitting the trail that we set that morning. After spending sixteen hours in a dust bowl of howling wind, we awoke to more of the same. We were dusty, cold, and ready to hit the trail in search of warmth, quiet air, and granite slabs. Even though it was early in the morning we looked like a well-oiled machine in action. All four of us stayed busy until the last bootlace was tied. Relentless wind, the kind that you have to yell over to hear each other, can bring out efficiency in the most reluctant worker.

Knowing how to pitch a tent, where it's safe to pitch a tent, what it takes to stay warm all night, how to get clean water, light the stove, cook dinner, and respect the wild places we were visiting are all skills that our kids developed, each day, as they watched, learned, and tried for themselves. The way one set up their tent mate's sleeping bag for them, just because; the way one prepared a snack for oneself, but made enough to share. We knew that it was all of these small moments of living that forged the real relationships.

Chapter 10

Trees

The forests of America, however slighted by man, must have been a great delight to God; for they were the best he ever planted... but he cannot save them from fools, only Uncle Sam can do that.
~ John Muir, 1897 [23]

Day 6: Gladys Lake to Devil's Postpile National Monument; 7 miles

Waking to a pleasant nip in the air triggered some discussion of the unusually chilly and windy days we were having. (We found out later that a near record-breaking cold front in California was passing through.) Despite our optimism that this strange weather would pass, the reality played out very differently than we had hoped it would.

We stepped on a brand new trail that day that would connect the dots between the areas we had hiked over the past few years, thus concluding the first leg of our trek.

When we hit the trail, we quickly saw trees blown down, everywhere. We had heard about the record blow down for weeks but never could have imagined the complete destruction these winds had caused. One massive tree after another, ripped out at its roots and toppled over on top of other massive trees—like Lincoln Logs—lined the trail. We marveled at the intense work the forestry crew must have put in to clear these thousands of trees downed over forty miles of trail.

All this catastrophic damage happened in ten hours on November 30, 2011, with the forest sustaining winds of 100 mph and gusts topping 190 mph. Normally, winds blow through the area in one direction and trees develop their root structure to defend against the familiar wind patterns. On the day of the storm, however, a surprise attack of hurricane force winds blew through from a completely different direction and the root structures holding down 400-year-old trees lost the fight.

John Muir's writings on the American forest speaks of their ancient charm. "It took more than three thousand years to make some of the trees in these Western woods—trees that are still standing in perfect strength and beauty, waving and singing in the mighty forests of the Sierra. Through all the wonderful, eventful centuries God has cared for these trees, saved them from drought, disease, avalanches, and a thousand straining, leveling tempests and floods…" [24]

At times the tone of our hike turned somber walking through this historic, living (or not living any longer) museum. Awe mixed with sadness as we saw the massive level of annihilation, the silent graveyard of sage old trees that had weathered countless years of storms caught off guard on one fateful day.

But perhaps sadness was misplaced. In my lifetime I will not see this forest return to what it was before November 30, 2011. However, the beauty of the wilderness is that it changes; what can look like death at first is really opening up pathways for new life. Landscapes changing over the millenniums are what shape the land beneath our feet and the soaring peaks that line the horizon. By the time we exited the trail, I made peace with the epic storm of November 30.

We made our way out at Red's Meadow to resupply, refresh, repack, and refocus for a few layover days in our trailer. Our first leg was an easy success, assuring our questioning minds that we could indeed do what we had set out to do. Bekah's blisters had healed. We had walked through gorgeous landscapes to relax at delightful lakes. We had hit a nice groove.

Perhaps, though, the ease of the first sixty miles gave us a false sense of security as what lay ahead was infinitely more challenging than what we left behind. We had hurdles to jump that we'd never had to jump before, making it handy that we could not see into the future. I'm not sure we could have handled knowing what was ahead. Taking life and long distance hikes one step at a time is the pace that works best anyway.

Thankfully, that's all the trail asks of us: one step at a time. This is the pace, after all, with which nature changes, transforms, ebbs, and flows. It's the only way it knows.

One moment at a time.

Chapter 11

Nature's Healing Power

*Keep close to Nature's heart... and break clear away, once in
awhile, and climb a mountain or spend a week in the woods.
Wash your spirit clean.*
~John Muir [25]

⊷⟩⟨⊶

Day 7: Rock Creek Trailhead to Trail Lake over Mono
Pass (12,000 ft.); 6 miles and 3200 ft. elevation change

The entry point to the next leg of our adventure marked
the beginning of the longest stretch I had ever spent on the
trail. Depending on how slow or fast we moved, our trip
would be from sixteen to nineteen days. We could only carry
five to six days of food, so we mailed food in orange Home
Depot buckets to two different drop spots along our path.

Why work so hard to just sit in nature? There is no
economic profit. No easy obvious gains. There is no
guarantee that nature will even cooperate. With only one to

two weeks to get away, maybe Mickey Mouse and his guaranteed clean, predictable, colorful world is the best use of time (and occasionally, it probably is). But I'd like to argue that to achieve a real deep down, cleansing sense of that "got away" feeling, we might need a touch of the unpredictability of nature.

You don't have to take my word for it, though. Research is pouring in from a growing field of "ecopsychology" that our disconnect from nature is stressing the human race.

The massive peaks that towered over the trail head and rushing stream that flowed beside the parking lot briefly made me wonder if it was that necessary to leave at all. Couldn't we just download the peace and biophilia while sitting on our tailgate eating organic berries? Researcher, Terry Hartig, PhD, MPH out of Uppsala University in Gavle, Sweden, actually found that, no, we have to work a little harder than that to get that prized focused, clear-headed buzz.

In comparing three groups in a series of lab and field experiments, he explored nature's ability to help people recover from what he calls "normal psychological wear and tear." After participants completed a forty-minute series of tasks designed to exhaust their directed attention capacity, he randomly assigned participants to either; 1, spend forty minutes walking in a local nature preserve; 2, spend forty minutes walking in an urban area; or 3, sit quietly while reading magazines and listening to music. The urban preserve walkers reported more positive emotions, less anger, and outperformed the other groups in a standard proofreading task. [26]

As for the impact on children, in the April 24, 2003, edition of *Cornell News*, Nancy Wells, assistant professor at the New York State College of Human Ecology reported that being close to nature, in general, helps boost a child's attention span. [27]

How can spending time with trees and dirt have the outcomes that Hartig and Wells are reporting? Dr. Stephen R. Kellert of Yale University explained it this way: that "play in nature, particularly during the critical period of middle childhood, appears to be an especially important time for developing the capacities for creativity, problem solving, and emotional and intellectual development." [28]

Taking it a step farther, Richard Louv asserted: "Time in nature is not leisure time; it's essential investment in our children's health (and also, by the way in our own)." [29] I can sense that something unseen, deep within each of our kids, is being stirred.

So back in to invest we went with high hopes, full packs, and fresh legs. We climbed over Mono Pass that first day, passing at least forty day-hikers in the first few stunning miles. Each pass of another hiker brought huge smiles when they saw two young kids with backpacks bouncing up the trail. A few comments from some of the older hikers of, "I love to see kids out here," stirred a desire in me to stop and ask them to tell me more. Why such huge smiles and surprised expressions? Weren't there lots of other kids farther up the trail, doing exactly what we were doing? As we walked through this wilderness, we discovered that if we, a family with young kids backpacking out here were a species, we'd be on the rare and endangered list. The only kid we passed on our entire journey was the child of friends of ours who surprised us and intersected our path as we headed out from Garnet Lake. Aaron and his family were on a quick three-night trip and loved every moment of it. Besides them, we never saw another kid.

Maybe this older hiking generation noticed what the research has found, that active kids out in nature are slowly waning. Busy families, video games, and the easy lure of the couch seem to be winning out in the fight for people's time. With the crazy pace the American family leads, vacations tend to be speed-window-sightseeing of beautiful places. It's breathless and often indoors. Sitting in a car is still inside. The car is outside, not its inhabitants. The car feels the warmth of the sun and the wind lashing the windows. No wonder dogs hang their heads out the window, straight into the wind. They crave what's on the other side of that glass. They want to smell every critter that has walked the miles that the car is flying past. They want to feel the coolness of the wind as it assaults their senses at 65 mph.

A few years ago, our favorite ranger, Ranger Jay Snow, who calls his home Death Valley National Park, told us a most poignant account of a father and his sons on vacation at the park. Ranger Jay's salt-and-pepper colored hair and strong lines on his sun-weathered face tell a story without saying a word: this man has spent many years exploring outside. His Oklahoma thick drawl and contagious energy make it impossible not to adore him. He has a characteristic jump that looks like a cross between a two-step swing dance move and the starting moments to an Olympian's 100-yard dash that always accompanies his high-pitched declaration that, "This place is ahhhhsuuuummmm! And you own this place! It's yours!" The beauty of Death Valley lies in the chasm between what is most obvious and that which is not obvious. Thousands of acres of ancient lake bed, uplifted rock, canyons, and 14,000 foot mountain peaks juxtapose the littlest details of life that require visitors to pause and pay attention. Being the driest and hottest place in America produces unique beauty that takes time and a quiet spirit to see. It's not the in-your-face kind of beauty of Yosemite National Park, yet it's beautiful all the same.

This being true, Ranger Jay could not believe what he witnessed when he came upon this family on one of those "drive-by" vacations so common to busy Americans. He had just ended another spectacular ranger led-hike through a curving, rugged canyon full of mysterious colorful layers of rocks and endless exploratory options. As Ranger Jay stooped down to climb into his sun-bleached faded blue Ford Escort to drive back to headquarters, he overheard a dad talking to his three children. "Kids, I'll be right back. I'm just stepping out for a second to get a picture."

"Dad, I want to get out and see!" protested one of his sons.

"Oh, no, guys. Just stay put. I'll show you the pictures when we get home."

Ranger Jay had to bite his tongue, wanting to holler in their direction, "Let your kids play in the dirt! Let them out! Let them touch the rock walls of the canyon and scramble up a few slopes!" He told us later he about fell over when he heard this dad keep his kids barricaded from the wonders of another American National Park.

We couldn't agree more with Ranger Jay. As challenging as lacking oxygen felt that first day, as we all listlessly clawed our way to over 12,000 feet to summit Mono Pass, at least we had experienced it fully. We had gotten dirty and tired. As we sat at camp watching the sun set and the quiet penetrate, I was deeply glad we did not window-speed-sight-see at the trailhead but instead, took the harder road, donned our packs, and headed in.

Robert Pyle, a conservation biologist and author invoked the evocative phrase, "the extinction of experience," to describe this trend toward the decline in people experiencing nature. He writes:

"Direct, personal contact with living things affects us in vital ways that vicarious experience can never replace. I believe that one of the greatest causes of the ecological crisis is the state of personal alienation from nature in which many [children] live. We lack a widespread sense of intimacy with the living world... The extinction of experience... implies a cycle of disaffection that can have disastrous consequences. As cities and metastasizing suburbs forsake their natural diversity, and their citizens grow more removed from personal contact with nature, awareness and appreciation retreat... So it goes... the extinction of experience sucking the life from the land, the intimacy from our connections." [30]

This intimacy in connecting to nature is part of why Ranger Jay loves his job. He used to be a clinical psychiatrist but has never looked back on his bank-account-reducing decision to teach visitors of national parks about the amazing gift they have in the millions of acres they own as American citizens. Talking to more than a couple of hundred people, he passionately said, "Get out of your cars and explore! We own 399 national parks, national monuments, and historical sites. These were hard to get but they are easy to lose. Take ownership!" As we spent a day with him hiking around Death Valley last year, he said, "Have your kids hike barefoot sometimes! Lay on the ground, with bare feet, and put your toes on the rough bark of a tree. Let every part of you feel, touch, smell, taste, see, and hear this place! It's ahhhhhhhhsuuuummm!!" That's primary experience.

In an era where more and more people are experiencing life second hand through the internet and TV, older generations must love to see kids being raised to get out and experience the world—like they did—directly. They love seeing young kids who are not experiencing nature through pictures online or on TV, but instead are sitting by streams and listening to them gurgle, sitting on rocks and watching the sunset and feeling the nip in the air, and listening to birds as they greet the day.

These are the kids who are having a genuine, "primary experience." In *The Necessity of Experience*, Edward Reed, who was an associate professor of psychology at Franklin and Marshall College, articulately questions a society that spends so much energy and money trying to make digital information available to everyone, but does "little or nothing to help us explore the world for ourselves." [31] One-way experiences through electronic media only requires the use of vision and hearing. This limited sensory phenomenon is replacing full sensory experiences.

In contrast, natural settings integrate informal play with formal learning in what Reed has coined "primary experiences," which is "the ability to experience our world directly." Sadly, this direct learning is losing popularity as we continue to plug in for our sensory fixes.

Our 200-mile summer was about discovering what these older Americans already knew, that we won't fight for something we don't know exists. This is a very real threat to our natural lands if our kids don't have at least the chance to fall in love with them. As long as we are plugged in we can turn a blind eye to the truth of our complete interconnectedness with a healthy planet.

And if a healthy planet is too obscure and granolaey for you, maybe a healthy body is closer to home. New studies have found that getting into nature actually does make us healthier. Depression and stress are drastically reduced when a consistent dose of nature is poured on the soul. According to Thomas Doherty, a clinical psychologist in Portland, Oregon, and the editor of *Ecopsychology*, there are quantifiably measurable benefits of nature for both body and mind: "In green spaces, for example, people's heart rates decrease, their muscles relax, and they become calmer. It's the difference you feel when you leave behind a busy city street for a peaceful park." [32]

Furthermore, exposure to nature may reduce the symptoms of Attention Deficit Hyperactive Disorder, as well as increase resistance to depression and stress in children. Frances E. Kuo, PhD, has tested nature's impact on middle-class children with ADHD. Parents reported that their children exhibited fewer symptoms after spending time in green surroundings than when they pursued activities indoors or in non-green outdoor areas. [33]

Some of the most important work in this area is coming out of the Human Environment Research Laboratory at the University of Illinois. Their recommendation to ADD kids: Go out and play! The greener the setting, the more the relief. The university's Landscape and Human Health Lab's research has shown that performing activities in green settings can reduce children's Attention Deficit-Hyperactivity Disorder symptoms. [34]

The sad reality is that all of this supportive research and even a catchy jingle about nature therapy does not stand a fighting chance over the latest antidepressant pharmaceuticals. The *Psychiatric Services* journal published their findings in 2003, stating that the rate at which American children are prescribed antidepressants increased by 49 percent over a five-year period. For the first time, spending on psychotropic drugs surpassed spending on antibiotics and asthma medications for children. [35]

But perhaps an inexpensive and just as feasible a treatment plan could simply be spending time in nature. Peter Kahn would agree as he summarized the findings of over one hundred studies in *The Human Relationship With Nature*, showing us that stress reduction is one of the main benefits of heading outside. [36]

Undeniably our children, not just adults, need this. It's worth the fight to get here.

Chapter 12

Setbacks

In the morning everything is joyous and bright... Innumerable insects begin to dance, the deer withdraw from the open glades and ridge tops to their leafy hiding places in the chaparral, the flowers open and straighten their petals as the dew vanishes, every pulse beats high, every life cell rejoices, the very rocks seem to tingle with life, and God is felt brooding over everything great and small.
~ *John Muir, 1894* [37]

Day 8: Trail Lake to Mono Lake Canyon, near Mono Creek

Some mornings back at home, as I scanned over different news sites, I wanted to either pound my fists in angry disbelief or shed a few tears. After the school shootings in Connecticut and the bombings at the Boston marathon, I actually did both. We can read about starving orphans in South America, wars in Syria, killings in New York, and terrorism in Afghanistan at the touch of a screen, all at the same time, almost in real time. Were we really created to be able to deal with that kind of onslaught? What can I do? I can vote. I can send aid money for heart-wrenching causes. I can help my neighbor build a fence. I can hug a sad child. But the news keeps rolling in. So if the wilderness is good for anything, it's good for giving our poor, tired, and weary minds a break from the NBC news blitz every day.

The campsite we woke to offered up the other side of life: the beautiful and serene. The revenge and hatred embodied in global news stories has no part on the wilderness stage. I needed some time to dance on that stage.

Our peaceful morning of birds chirping and squirrels scampering quickly shifted gears when Cade—our super athlete, always moving fast, never sick, always smiling, super boy—began complaining of a stomach ache from his tent. He had been unusually tired the night before as we climbed over that 12,000-foot pass—2000 feet of elevation change over about five miles of hiking, starting at 2:00 on a hot afternoon. Then I watched him scarf down his granola in classic Cade form, and happily went about my morning chores, content to believe the stomach issue had passed. Cade seemed like his usual, fast-moving self.

Within a short time, he started complaining of his stomach hurting even worse. Hoping it would relieve shortly, we tried to get him to relax and drink some water. Mistake number one had been the lack of water he had consumed climbing the pass. He woke up dehydrated and drinking water shocked his system, causing the pain to increase at an alarming rate. He clutched his stomach and draped himself over a four-foot boulder, immoveable, moaning and crying.

My mind flashed back to the week earlier when our friends camped with us at our California hideout. They all got sick, throwing up and feeling generally rotten, but we had chalked it up to altitude sickness. Many folks who go from sea level to 10,000 feet in a matter of a couple of days suffer exactly like they did.

The kink in our theory came two days after their misery when Bekah clutched her stomach in pain. Crazily enough, we explained it away, having fed her a huge banana split with sugary/corn syrup laden sorbet.

"She simply overate, right? She never eats corn syrup, let alone that much of it." I had said to my concerned husband. "Let me give her some Pepto Bismol." The pink promise of pain relief gagged her almost instantly and resulted in her first vomiting experience in her life. When she threw up again an hour later, we suspected that our friends' altitude sickness might be contagious, meaning it wasn't altitude sickness at all. Maybe it was a virus?

We delayed our trip a day to make sure a virus was not running rampant, as that is no way to start a 100-mile thru-hike.

So as we now watched and helped Cade, who was convinced he was dying, we suddenly didn't know if we should hike out or hike on.

The debate began with Cory. "If it's altitude, hiking out would be very difficult since we have to gain elevation to get over Mono Pass again."

I jumped to the worst-case scenario, like I often do. "I am 97 percent sure this has to be a virus—so Bekah throwing up a few days ago must have been the same thing and there's no way I want to be out here sick and throwing up!"

"Yeah, but if we get sick, we get sick. We might not. And if this is altitude sickness it could actually be dangerous to climb those 1000 feet to get over the pass."

Seconds later, Cade moaned dramatically and cried out in greater urgency, "This is horrible!"

"Geez, maybe he is just sick. Should we hike back to the truck? Maybe we should wait it out here and head over the pass this afternoon," Cory proposed.

We tried to get Cade to sit up and drink a little more water, but he refused to let go of the large boulder he had draped himself over.

"No, I really think we need to get him down in elevation. From this campsite, it's downhill all the way to Vermillion Valley Ranch where we can recoup at 7,500 feet. This must be altitude sickness," Cory determined.

Efficiently we divvied out his pack items to the rest of us so his pack was little more than some high-tech material draping from his shoulders, helped him put his shoes on, offered him more water, and pulled him to his shaky feet.

Cade looked like a newborn deer attempting to take its first steps. He was pale and miserable, and upon standing on shaky legs that barely allowed him to stay erect, he quickly threw up.

The debate waged on. Bekah had never thrown up before and Cade had never had altitude sickness and yet we had two bouts of vomit in four days. Seemed like a virus had hit the clan and we were at a loss as to how to proceed. Hundreds of dollars of food was waiting for us at two different drop spots down the trail. We had planned, dreamed, and prepared for months, and we had family coming down from Oregon to shuttle us from the trailhead we were heading towards out to resupply and then back to the trailhead to keep going. Did we really have to abort the trip?

Cory stayed firm in his resolve that Cade was suffering from altitude sickness and felt that the best plan was to march forward, as it was the only option we had that took us downhill. It was a surprising turn of events because Cade had already spent plenty of time at altitude during our last leg, just days earlier. We learned later from many hikers that altitude sickness could strike anyone, anytime, anywhere, even if you think you are acclimatized. Hiking down towards VVR, a mountain hiker's resort that was in our route as our next resupply point seemed like the safest thing to do. Worse case scenario of Cade actually having a virus would mean we would have to stay longer at VVR to let him recuperate but best case scenario meant that within a few hours of hiking to lower elevations we would see him recover quickly.

We started hiking down, down, down until we reached Golden Stream where Cade begged for a nap. We stopped and let him nap for what we thought would be a half an hour. I am very sensitive to altitude, too, and have found an easy way for me to overcome it is to nap. In the weeks that I am acclimatizing, I often get extremely tired in the early afternoon. It's the kind of tired that hits hard and fast and allows for no other options but sleep. If I can sleep for twenty minutes, I wake up refreshed. Within a few weeks of this pattern, the need to nap wears off. Soon, I can make it the entire day without resting.

Twenty minutes extended into two hours that passed slowly while Cade continued to sleep. The three of us waited, worried about how sick Cade really was and wondering who would be next. Did we make the wrong choice? The trailhead was now even farther from where we were waiting, with 1000 feet of climbing and seven miles of walking between us and our truck.

He woke up groggy and only slightly improved. I noticed that I felt nauseous myself. Was it real or was it a mother's sympathy pains? He took his time in getting up.

"Cade, can you hike?" I asked.

"Yeah, I feel a little better." Such courage, I thought.

We loaded our packs onto our backs and hiked on— down, down, down we went. By the time we reached a lunch spot, we were at 8,500 ft, plenty of elevation change to bring relief to someone dealing with altitude sickness. Cade dipped his hiking hat in the water, put it on his head, and declared that he was feeling 97 percent better.

From "near death" to "near perfect" in half a day did not speak of a virus. His rebound was remarkable, but also a classic textbook case of altitude sickness where drinking water, napping, and getting to lower elevations resulted in a quick improvement.

The stress of the day knocked the appetite right out of Cory and me. Helplessly watching our son feel so wretched far away from the comforts of home—and wondering if we were next—made for a morose day.

We got into camp and went forward with the plans as normal; unpacking the backpacks and rehydrating our meat stew that I had made six weeks earlier. Cade, now feeling 100 percent, discovered a damp sleeping bag. Alarmed, we soon determined that his Platypus water bag had sprouted a leak (suddenly their lifetime warranty made no difference!) Keeping warm and dry is one of those critical-for-survival details that had just been jeopardized. We laid his bag out to dry and earmarked his water bag to repair it the next day. Surely this would not be counted as our favorite day of the summer.

As the evening approached we encountered our first mosquitoes. They came in swarms, blood-thirsty and aggressive. There would be no sitting that night. With a mosquito invasion like that one can either hop around trying to avoid them, swatting and squirming all evening or one could take cover inside their tent. I dove inside the tent while Cory braved the pesky buggers and worked on dinner.

The final blow of the day came while we all paced in camp, dodging mosquito attacks as we were attempting to eat. We were mid-bite when Cory abruptly halted dinner. "Everyone, stop eating! I think the meat is rancid. I just don't trust it." He sniffed it a few more times and concluded that for sure, the meat had gone bad.

Though I don't advocate cursing, this is the kind of day that deserved it.

Honestly, my stomach was so nervous and stressed from the craziness of the day that I had little use for food, so it wasn't a big deal, but normally, our appetites are ferocious and we would have wanted to murder anyone who got between our mouths and our food. Ready to just go to sleep and try again the next day, we all just gave up and went to bed.

New mercies often come in the morning so we went to bed with a belief that the next day would be better. It had to be better! As we closed our eyes that night with high hopes, we had no way of knowing what might be in store for us when the sun peeked over the horizon the next morning.

Chapter 13

The Oasis

Unless someone like you cares a whole awful lot,
Nothing is going to get better. It's not.
~ Dr. Seuss, *The Lorax*

⤳⁀⸜⸝

Day 9: The forest to Vermillion Valley Ranch; 11 miles

After a day with a commode-hugging son, discovering a leaky water bottle and wet sleeping bag, and a rancid dinner, we approached the next morning with unusual caution. Cade's rough start changed our route and cut out a two day trek up into the gorgeous high basin of Laurell Lakes.

We had hardly earned a break as we had only been out for three days, but the day's plans included a hike to Edison Lake where we would catch a ferry across the five-mile reservoir to the one resort we would stay at all summer. It really is about putting one foot in front of the next, come heck or high water, with a good attitude, a healthy dose of faith, and as good of common sense as possible. It also doesn't hurt to have tasty power bars! Armed with chocolate and smiles, we hit the trail.

A warm downhill hike along Mono Creek was the perfect healing balm to my nerves from the day before. Despite the mosquitoes, I was amazed that a walk along a river never fails to inspire. Fears were reorganized into a healthy perspective. I noticed our confidence and joy of being outside returning with each step we took. Something about gurgling water with golden sun beams dancing across the surface consistently makes edginess dissolve.

As we hiked, we got warmer with each incremental drop in elevation. After a few hours on a hot dusty trail, water crossings became highlights. A simple stream elicited the hoots and hollers equivalent to an announcement of a pizza party. We splashed our faces with refreshing water. We had air conditioning for miles in the form of soaked hats and bandannas draped on our hot heads. We refilled our water bottles, but not before subjecting them to the ultraviolet purification of the Steripen, which dutifully kills viruses, giardia, and cryptosporidium. While an estimated 50 percent of the hikers in the California Sierra range drink straight from the streams, we chose a more conservative route and subjected all our water to purification.

After a few miles, we ran into three men who informed us that the ferry across the lake had stopped running for the year due to low water levels, following a record low snow year. Some of the benefits of this record-breaking dry year were the pleasing low levels of mosquitoes at higher altitudes, easy stream crossings, and no snow packs to cross. But that also meant that there was not enough water in the lake, so our five-mile easy day turned into a long, hot eleven-mile day.

Actually, the hike along the lake was delightful. I always love to hike when I can see water and looking out across a large body of sparkling water was a refreshing change of pace to the miles of dark forest we had just left behind.

At lunch, as we sat on boulders and gazed out over the reservoired lake, surrounded by tree stumps and acres and acres of exposed beach that normally would have been covered by water, we started a discussion with the question, "Should the State of California have dammed this river?" Ideas came forth from all four of us, for and against it. Truly, in comparison to the raw beauty of the land farther up the creek, out of the destructive reach of the dam, this lake was an eyesore. Stumps lined the shore, acres of sand existed where there once was a lush forest, but the very dried apricots we were eating were the result of this very water that irrigated the California agricultural lands and provided electricity to dehydrate them in a factory.

We divided into two teams, each team taking either a pro or con side. It was amazing to look at this seemingly simple question from many directions and I found myself floating between pro and con with every good idea that came forth. At minimum, it reminded me of the importance of being open-minded to the many perspectives that exist on issues. Narrow mindedness builds walls, not bridges. As we sat on that boulder that day engaged in discussion, I hoped our children would see that their opinions mattered, that they would be open to other points of view, and would reach viable conclusions that allow us to work together, instead of fight.

We had no idea that the water we sat near contributed what it could to the Big Creek System to deliver power to 4.3 million customers throughout California, producing 1,000 megawatts of power an hour. Edison Power company proudly declares: "For over 100 years... life. Powered by Edison." [39]

We found out later that Edison Lake is just one lake in the Big Creek System that is comprised of six major reservoirs, twenty-seven dams, nine powerhouses, and miles of interconnecting infrastructure earning it the motto, "The Hardest Working Water in the World." [40]

We hiked on to our destination, and like an oasis in a desert, the Vermillion Valley Ranch sign appeared. VVR had a small town feel with a staff that sought to know each person who passed through their front door. It was a convergence of those who drove in to sleep in cabins or trailers and those who arrived by foot (which is the majority), seeking a night to refresh.

With a cabana-type indoor/outdoor restaurant and a sign over the front door that said, "Hikers! Please loiter!" the stage was set for people from all walks of life to gather and chat over coffee, beer, or the evening fire pit. And that is exactly what we did. Whether we talked with the seasonal staff, the trailer fisherman, or a fellow hiker, the continual theme was the critical need each person had to get away and deeply relax, and how being in a peaceful and quiet forested Sierra natural landscape—like we all found ourselves—was the best way we all knew.

"I could never miss my yearly fishing trip up here," said an older man with a bushy white beard and overalls one night around the campfire.

We each found a way to cross paths with nature differently—some with a fly rod in hand, others with packs on their backs, still others in lawn chairs on the porch of their rented cabins—but we all experienced what the research had determined… that connecting with nature affects us deeply—spiritually, physically, and emotionally, serving to recharge and restore us in profound ways.

VVR had rustic and simple accommodations, but to us, it was perfect paradise. A little bell rang on the creaky wooden door of the store as we stepped over the threshold to check in. Jim, the friendly owner of the ranch, greeted us and got our tab started. The first thing we put on it was their last available room. Room number 4 had three beds, a shower, and a kitchenette. For twenty-four hours we lived a luxurious life again with hot tea in real mugs, hot showers, an actual table to have our meals, and the most comfortable beds I had ever slept on.

Pinning our laundry on a line to dry, I couldn't stop smiling at the simple sweetness of clean smelling, newly laundered clothes. Backpacking has a miraculous way of making simple comforts feel like an ultimate spoiling. It was nice to appreciate these things again. I needed to remember to do this even when life barely allowed me to breathe between meetings and deadlines; soft beds, a roof over our heads, and warm showers were gifts to be grateful for. Time with friends and family, health, and a large bowl of raw greens all are treasures to savor.

I smiled as Cade and Bekah also squealed in delight over simple luxuries upon returning to civilization. Trail time had awakened in them a deeper awareness of their surroundings. It had replaced entitlement with gratitude.

For months after our arrival back home, Cade and Bekah would spontaneously exclaim, "Don't you just love the feeling of carpet?" or "I love my bed!" or "It's so easy to drink water —just turn on the faucet!"

More than just to be somewhere to indulge, we were at VVR to pick up our two resupply buckets with the food we needed for the next six nights. As we ambled around the ranch doing various tasks, random hikers arrived bringing stories of their current and past experiences on the trail. All in all, it was a perfect day. We had arrived at an oasis in the wilderness.

How could we ever leave this place?

Chapter 14

Layover days

The tendency nowadays to wander in wildernesses is delightful to see.

~ John Muir, 1901 [41]

❧

Day 10: A layover day at VVR

There is probably no nicer way to wake up than to be in an extremely comfortable bed, on vacation, without an agenda for the day. Precious few days do I wake up knowing that I don't have a large task list for either my mind to pursue or my body to tackle. But on this day when I woke up, I laid in bed thinking, "Can I really do whatever I want to do today?" We had a few water bags to repair and our resupply buckets to sort through and pack into our bear canisters, but other than that, we were free to sit around the ranch read, journal, and talk with the constant stream of JMTers and PCTers who randomly appeared throughout the day at the camp store.

We ate lunch with a seventy-three-year-old man, nicknamed Kiwi Yellowshirt, who spoke with a New Zealand accent (hence the trail name Kiwi) of all the peaks he had climbed and trips he had taken. His skin was tan and weathered from the obvious time this man had lived outside. His hands were strong and his legs were sturdy. Stories of near-death moments, stubborn peaks to summit, and long traverses spilled out of this man, full of life and ready to go. Six months out from a titanium knee replacement was not keeping him from the trail. "My physical therapist would kill me if he knew I was out here hiking the JMT. But it's not so bad. My leg with the titanium knee pulls my other bad leg down the trail."

A year later, in the same spot in the country store where Kiwi had inspired us with his stories, I met Whitney. The first thing Whitney said to me was, "Which color should I get?" as she held out a green and a brown VVR shirt in my direction. I turned around to the energetic voice behind me to see a spunky gal in her early thirties, with a brown ponytail under a blue bandana. Her spark and energy immediately bonded us. The VVR country store attracts the most amazing people to it for sure. I have met quite a few life-time friends there while gathering a few items needed for the trail.

"I'm a green-loving girl. I'd say green. I'm Julie."

"Whitney. Green, huh? Okay, I agree. It's earthy."

"Are you hiking the JMT?"

"Yeah. My husband and I are. It's not going so good, though. We lost a day when we decided to come here, but this guy Peter we met on the trail encouraged us because my knee has been hurting so much."

"Peter?" As my voice trailed off, I looked up to see none other than Kiwi walking into the store. I called out, "No way, Peter! I can't believe you are here! How long are you staying?"

He looked over at me, taking a moment to recognize me.

I helped him out. "We met you here last year. You emailed us a few months ago asking if we could plan a trip together this summer but it didn't work out. What are the chances?" Some people you were just meant to know, and Mr. Kiwi was one of them.

"Oh, yes. I remember! Cory and Julie, right?"

"Yep. That's us!"

"I'm staying for two nights. How about you guys?"

"Two nights as well. Once you get settled, come on over to room number 4!"

"Sounds good!" He turned toward a younger man who I assumed was Whitney's husband.

I took the break in our conversation to turn back to Whitney. "You know while you are here, you can do laundry?"

"That sounds good, but I need a shower! I can't think straight until I get a shower!"

We parted ways but met up again in the laundry room twenty minutes later. She stuffed clothes into the washing machine as I loaded mine into the dryer. Suddenly she looked up with a dirty sock in her hand and said, "My husband is not a good hiking partner. He's so negative! He's a doctor, and everything has to be so predictable and laid out. When things don't go perfectly as planned, he gets so wigged out. Damn it! I'm here to seize the moment, take what comes and love that. He's just driving me crazy!"

This soap-box speech sealed the deal; I instantly loved this new spirited friend. We talked for a long time with the roar of the machines forcing our conversation to be loud and animated.

An hour later, Peter came over to our room. We convened at the picnic table on our room's porch. My ears were still ringing from my laundry room conversation as I settled into my chair opposite the quiet-spoken, jazz radio announcing soothing voice of Peter. Over a chilled microbrew, he said in his strong New Zealand accent, "I got my second knee in January, six months ago." This would have kept most seventy-four-year-old American men on the couch with a TV remote in hand, but all it did for Kiwi was cause him to change his trail name to the Tinman.

For two days my thirty-nine-year-old husband chatted, studied maps, and shared trail stories with a man twice his age who totally "got" him. They both got excited about topography lines that held the secrets to less-traveled cross-country routes and talked with enthusiasm about their chosen gear. Because their voices stayed subdued and understated, an observer might miss the passion these two had for their Sierra mountains. Cory all but sat at this living legend's feet, hearing stories of trails we had yet to explore. As I watched them staring at a map together like two eight-year-olds in a candy shop, I saw a twinkle in both their eyes; staring at those maps was staring at home.

Later we shared a booth at the VVR restaurant and a bottle of wine with Peter-the Tinman, Whitney and Matthew. We compared notes on our hiking partners and found that our husbands didn't understand our '3:30 is quitting time' hiking mantra.

"Whitney is absolutely predictable. A few days ago, she literally fell over on the trail, looked up at me and said, 'I'm done. Not moving. We're camping here.' I told her we couldn't camp there, we were on the trail and a few hikers were heading our way. They kindly just sort of stepped around her as she assured me she was not moving," said Matthew.

"Hey, I get that! 3:30 is quitting time. Period. If we are hiking at 3:32 I start to get really grumpy and cranky and blame all my life problems on Cory. If we aren't relaxing at a sunny campsite by 3:30, then he becomes the reason for everything bad and evil. Even the Iraq war is his fault if we aren't done on time," I said to the laughing crowd. And on it went into the night in a mountain resort without phone reception or wifi.

The next morning we bid farewell to Whitney and Matthew. They hitched a ride to the trailhead in an old VVR white dog-catcher van with a steel gate separating the surly-looking driver's compartment from the passengers. I wondered if they were prisoners or hikers. Would they even make it to the trailhead?

Two weeks later I received a text that included a picture of Whitney with her hands high in the air on top of her namesake mountain, and I had my answer. The caption on this victory shot read, "My life has been forever changed."

Hikers like the Tinman, Whitney, and Matthew might have been weary, sore, and craving a cold microbrew, but they all had one thing in common: they, like us, could not resist the trail. Why?

The energizing conversations in this newly forming community of friends was part of what fed my love of hiking. I loved the people we met. The stories we swapped. The challenges and victories that we shared. Sitting on the bench outside the country store, I spent most of the afternoon in conversation with the people of this world. All walks of life were represented, as under the great expanse of the sky, surrounded by trees, we were all part of humanity. It mattered little what we all did when not on the trail. Single unemployed men from Denmark could talk as equals (because they were) with well-to-do doctors from San Francisco. The charm of the trail was the community that formed where suddenly who I was was more important than what I did. In fact, what any of us did off trail was no longer connected—as it shouldn't have been—with who we were.

As I moved about the ranch, chatting with fellow travelers, many questions were asked of us. "How do you motivate your kids to hike out here?" came from a couple who had donned their packs but left their kids at home. The answer was slowly taking shape as we took on each day, but at that point in our journey my answer to them was to just try. Start young. Don't give up.

As each day passed, the answer became even clearer. Just as contagious as the energy buzz was when we adult hikers congregated in front of VVR's rustic country store to swap stories, victories, and defeats, it seemed to be for our kids as well. Once they got past the dull work it took to lug a pack down a trail, they got into the adventure of it, just as we did.

Their excitement propelled them to turn another corner and watch more landscape unfold in front of them, as well as discover the unique ways nature could assist them—whether it be a perfectly shaped sitting rock at lunch, a large shade tree for an afternoon nap, or a cold stream for a refreshing splash in the morning.

Like us, they loved looking back and seeing how far their own legs had taken them. They were inspired by trading in walls for the freedom and fantasy of nature. In some ways, it wasn't difficult at all to get the kids out there. They naturally yearned for open space.

With T-shirts, stickers, mugs, and magnets for sale, all declaring the triumphant accomplishment of hiking the JMT, I realized this dream of ours was part of an historic pilgrimage, as important to us as the Spanish pilgrimage, El Camino de Santiago, was and still is to others. I felt disappointed that our 200 plus miles were not the exact 204 miles that make up the JMT. Our constraints required our own creative version of trails to connect Yosemite National Park to Kings Canyon National Park. It was beautiful and stunning and difficult but I had not earned the t-shirt.

Sometimes the real reason any of us hiked the JMT was because it was there for the hiking. Some pilgrims hiked it once, some, like The Tinman, hiked it every year. Some people, of course, never feel called to do it at all. But since 1938 when the final section, the Golden Staircase was completed, the JMT remains a pilgrimage for any and all. And we will do it! Some summer soon, our 204 miles will be the exact footprint of the entire JMT.

In 1884, Theodore Solomons was the first to have the vision of a high-elevation trail, passable by stock, that followed the spine of the Sierra from Yosemite Valley to Kings Canyon. He was only fourteen. "The idea of a crest-parallel trail through the High Sierra came to me one day while herding my uncle's cattle in an immense, unfenced alfalfa field near Fresno," he wrote in the *Sierra Club Bulletin* in 1940.

Solomon's vision created the most beautiful trail in America. Winding through three national parks, two wilderness areas, and a national monument, the JMT is one of the premier hiking trails in the country.

By the late 1800s, stressed city dwellers were discovering the wilderness as John Muir noted in his 1901 book, *Our National Parks*, "Thousands of tired, nerve-shaken, over-civilized people are beginning to find out that going to the mountains is going home; that wildness is a necessity; and that mountain parks and reservations are useful not only as fountains of timber and irrigating rivers, but as fountains of life. Awakening from the stupefying effects of the vice of over-industry and the deadly apathy of luxury, they are trying as best they can to mix and enrich their own little ongoings with those of Nature, and to get rid of rust and disease. Briskly venturing and roaming, some are washing off sins and cobweb cares of the devil's spinning in all-day storms on mountains; sauntering in rosiny pinewoods or in gentian meadows, brushing through chaparral, bending down and parting sweet, flowery sprays; tracing rivers to their sources, getting in touch with the nerves of Mother Earth; jumping from rock to rock, feeling the life of them, learning the songs of them, panting in whole-souled exercise, and rejoicing in deep, long-drawn breaths of pure wildness". [42]

Saving the Silver Divide and Forester Pass for a future trip was not because of difficulty, but rather from our safety concerns of tackling exposed trail with a nine-year-old girl who is less mule-like and sure-footed than we'd like her to be. We created our own 200-mile summer, spending about 100 of those miles on the JMT, rounding out the remaining miles with less traveled basins. Discovering our own path through these mountains while creating our own connections between basins had its own charm; it was not all written about in a travel guide. But the lure to attempt the official JMT was never stronger than when we spent two days intersecting with stoked thru-hikers. Somehow, our 200 miles seemed "less than" to me.

Maybe as a way to break us of our first night's luxury stay in our most comfortable room number 4, there was nothing available in the inn for our second night. We were relegated to pitch our tent in the dusty, free-for-hikers, group camping area across the dirt road from the VVR store. We timed our stay in this crowded 300 square foot area perfectly so that we stayed with the most crude group on the trail. The night sounds of owls and coyotes were overshadowed by snorts, snoring, hacking, coughing, and yes, farting. Lovely.

One particularly talented man in the art of bodily noises had a most memorable chain of events that started with a loud burp, went straight into hacking, which morphed into a coughing fit, was dotted with snorts and grunts, and ended in a loud fart. It was about eleven p.m. when his body exploded in all of these directions at once, jolting our dozing minds awake. When he finished his performance, he loudly proclaimed, "Shit!" as I think even he was surprised, or maybe he was just plain impressed with himself. The last thing I heard before I was finally asleep for the night was Cory chuckling in his sleeping bag.

Leaving this dusty commune wasn't so hard after all. The charm of VVR had begun to wear off, just in time to kick us out of the nest and back into the pristine wilderness. And not knowing what lay ahead made for a buzz of anticipation as we lay in our sleeping bags, dreaming of what was to come, with a symphony of bodily noises resounding from nearby tents all around us.

Chapter 15

Kick the Digital Fix

... every crystal, every flower a window opening into heaven, a
mirror reflecting the Creator. From garden to garden, ridge to
ridge, I drifted enchanted...
~ John Muir's Journal entry for July 26, 1869 [43]

Day 11: VVR to Middle of Bear Creek Drainage; 8 miles,
1500 ft. elevation change

There's a school in the heart of the Silicon Valley that is
full of colored chalk, knitting needles, crayons, pens, paper,
and occasionally mud. What you won't find is a single
computer. This Waldorf school even frowns upon screen
time at home. Who sends their kids there? Surprise: three
quarters of the parents work in high-tech companies, such as
Google, Apple, Yahoo, and Hewlett-Packard. The chief
technology officer of eBay sends his children there.

The thinking is that technology interferes with creativity
and young minds learn best through movement, hands-on

tasks, and human-to-human interaction. Mr. Eagle, is an executive in communications at Google. With a computer science degree from Dartmouth, he knows a bit about technology. In an interview with the *New York Times,* he said that children will have plenty of time to learn computer skills. "It's super easy. It's like learning to use toothpaste. At Google and all these places, we make technology as brain-dead easy to use as possible. There's no reason why kids can't figure it out when they get older."

As students crisscross their wooden needles around balls of yarn, they are developing coordination, patterning, and problem-solving skills, and ultimately learning math. The process does not involve math computer games on a screen and the product is not a correctly filled-in worksheet. Instead, the process involves cutting up food into halves and quarters and creating fabric swatches. The product: well-formed knitted socks. Sounds more like summer camp than school, but at a price tag of nearly $20,000 per year, parents must believe it's working. In Los Altos, as well as over 150 similar schools across the country, parents say the Waldorf method works and they're sending their kids to top colleges, from Oberlin to Berkeley to Vassar.

As a teacher and mom, I walked those trails wondering where the kids of our world were. Perhaps Paul, a fourth grader in San Diego who responded to a survey from Richard Louv[44], sheds the biggest clue: "I like to play indoors better, 'cause that's where all the electrical outlets are." That might be true for Paul, but the Waldorf students have been allowed to discover the excitement of wondering, creating, and playing in mud and find themselves getting frustrated with their contemporaries who don't know how to play. One Waldorf student, Aurad, eleven, spoke of visiting his cousins and sitting around waiting for all five of them to stop playing with their gadgets. They weren't paying attention to him or to each other and he was the only child in the mix who had experienced something other than the digital world as their entertainment. He started waving his arms at them saying, "Hello, guys, I'm here."

Without a constant stream of TV and video games flashing before their eyes, these kids have been given an open slate to create their own fantasy worlds. A childhood like this produces very imaginative kids.

A friend told us of his godson who grew up with a technology-obsessed dad. "My boy's gonna have all the advantages I can provide him," this dad said of his two-year-old son. "I put a mouse in his hand as soon as he could understand how to use it." And sure enough, this godson, named John East, clicked away like a pro by the time he was two. Over the years our friend watched John retreat more and more into the world of computers. A visit to their house when John was in his early teens was utterly frustrating; John barely even mumbled a greeting as his mouse-adept hand clicked away on the computer.

Some years later, my friend ran into John East sitting at the registration booth of a Boy Scout Camp. "Are you *the* John East?" my friend asked the then, nineteen-year-old boy sitting at the table.

"Well, I am *a* John East. Not sure if I am *the* John East!" He quipped, uncharacteristic of the personality-less, computer-obsessed days of his teen years. John made friendly eye contact and actually carried on a witty conversation with my friend. A complete 180 degree change in him. Why?

John explained it this way. "I joined the Boy Scouts and felt myself come to life with every hike we took and every outing I went on. I hardly touch the computer these days! I am too busy living my life!" He chuckled.

My friend said that John was indeed a different person. He had light in his eyes. For the first time in his life, he was capable of conversation. He looked happy.

As we strolled along on the trail, completely content, I smiled as I realized how exciting and interesting and fun our kids' lives were unattached to video games and TV, just as John East had discovered.

Not watching TV just made sense with our busy schedule of park time, play groups, library time, and open play at home, which is exactly the advice given by the American Academy of Pediatricians: children under two should not spend time in front of a screen. Between built-in DVD players in mini-vans, iPhones, iPads, and handheld gaming systems, our American child is bombarded with screens around every corner. Even babies know how to swipe on an iPad and honestly, they shouldn't. It's an easy babysitter but it's replacing their interactions with the 3D world around them.

Passing exquisite mountain scenery in Yosemite, California, one summer, I noticed some kids sitting in the back seat of a designer SUV cruising down the highway alongside us. These elementary-aged kids stared, unwaveringly, at the seats in front of them. While the most celebrated national park stood tall in all its glory right outside their windows, these kids missed it. They were mesmerized by what flashed before their eyes on their own personal flat screen TVs.

Many parents will make sure that their kids always have a digital screen in front of their children during any open space times, willing to do almost anything to avoid hearing two words. And kids know it. What are these two words?

I'm bored.

"Quick, Johnny's bored… " and with that, the scramble to fix the mini crisis begins.

Instead of panicking, how about doing nothing at all? Dr. Laura Markham, a clinical psychologist at Columbia University, cautions parents from using technological innovations or structured activities to combat boredom. "Children need to encounter and engage with the raw stuff that life is made of: unstructured time." [45]

I love author Nancy H. Blakey's take on boredom: "It is a mistake to use television and organized activities as an antidote to boredom, for they devour precious time better spent claiming their imaginations, for in the end, that is all we have. There is little life beyond our imagining. If a thing cannot be imagined first—a cake, a relationship, a cure for AIDS—it cannot be. Our lives are inextricably bound by what we can envision. As we move through the human cycle it is possible for boredom to deliver us to our best selves. The self that longs for risk and illumination and unspeakable beauty. If we sit still long enough, we may hear the call behind boredom. With practice, we may have the imagination to rise up from the emptiness and answer it." [46]

A decade's worth of new studies on the negative effects of TV on learning, thinking, language skills, mood, and behavior underscore the recommendations made from the AAP in their November 2011 published policy statement in *Pediatrics: Official Journal of the American Academy of Pediatrics.* That statement stressed to pediatricians and parents the "importance of unstructured, unplugged play in allowing a child's mind to grow, problem-solve, think innovatively, and develop reasoning skills." [47]

Watching TV, playing video games, or spending time on the computer are in and of themselves not the problem. It's necessary for our children to know their way around this electronic world. The question is, does it characterize our child's day? Does it characterize our day? Are our kids' habits consistent with the findings by The Kaiser Family Foundation that, "kids under age six watch an average of about two hours of screen media a day, primarily TV and videos or DVD."

And even more alarming are their findings for kids and teens ages eight- to eighteen-years-old. They "average 7 hours and 38 minutes for using entertainment media across a typical day (more than 53 hours a week). And because they spend so much of that time 'media multitasking' (using more than one medium at a time), they actually manage to pack a total of 10 hours and 45 minutes worth of media content into those 7½ hours." [48]

This generation is consuming media for more hours a week than working a full time job does. Putting two and two together, if research supports unplugged time as the best way to allow children to develop and grow into innovative people, we have ourselves a real crisis. A generation of children who need to be plugged in to avoid that dreaded "bored" feeling is potentially going to produce a generation that has lost their natural inclination toward creativity: filling in their free time with their own imaginary play.

And taking this a step further, plugged-in kids are not outside. Biophilia has been booted to remedy boredom.

Talking with parents who can't keep their kids' interest when on a trail always admit that their children do spend a lot of time on the computer, watching TV, and playing video games. These digital babysitters are not only addictive, they dull our senses, slow our metabolism, and slowly kill the mind's ability to entertain itself. Their lure to prevent boredom breeds more boredom in the never-ending pursuit of another media fix.

The most complete study of TV habit and addiction comes from researchers Robert Kubey, a professor at Rutgers University and director of the Center for Media Studies, and Mihaly Csikszentmihalyi, professor of psychology at Claremont Graduate University. His conclusions in his paper, "Television Dependence, Diagnosis, and Prevention," make perfect sense. "Television watching is not an 'experience' but instead it replaces experiences. So TV watchers exchange the real world for the virtual one behind the screen." [49]

Why would we want to replace real experiences? Because doing so is relaxing. It's so relaxing that within sixty seconds of turning the tube on, our brain seems to turn off. In our fast-paced, stressed-out lifestyles, hooking up to a machine that can placate our brains and relieve us of thinking is enticing.

It's also addictive. It's a legal and effective way to escape from negative moods such as loneliness, sadness, anxiety, and anger. [50]

When the creators of these entertaining flashes of light do all the work for us, our metabolism knows it can downshift. Studies have found that our metabolism is slower while we watch TV than it is if we are sitting on that same couch, doing nothing. [51]

When we are awake and focused on something, our brains exhibit beta waves. If we meditate or relax, our brains move into an alpha wave pattern. When we drift off to sleep our brains exhibit delta waves. What waves flow through our brains as we stare at a TV? You guessed it: slow alpha waves fluctuating with delta waves. Watching television has the same effect on the brain as staring at a blank wall.

Part of what made this summer possible with our kids was that they weren't wishing they could go home to hook back up to their digital life line - we don't even own a television or a gaming system. They knew how to experience their world, first hand, and knew that their world didn't lack because it wasn't flashing and dancing in full digital color in front of them.

It's more than enough, it's invigorating. It's enchanting.

Chapter 16

Fully Alive

How complete is the absorption of one's life into the spirit of
mountain woods!
~ John Muir, Letter to Jeanne C. Carr, Undated, estimated as
September, 1874 [52]

Day 12: Middle of Bear Creek Drainage to Sandpiper
Lake; 8 miles, uphill

Cade's riverside sponge down turned into a full swim. He
greeted the cold water with his usual cautious, first-born
style. Never intending to actually swim, he slowly tested out
the water. One toe turned into the whole foot, which turned
into the other foot, which led to walking in to the knees,
which slowly led to both thighs before he decided it was not
unbearably cold and the current was not overwhelmingly fast.
No bigger smile had crossed his face all summer than the
moment when his head popped up out of the water for air, all
of his senses fully alive, his eyes sparkling bright.

The question so many had asked us—"How do we get our kids to backpack?"—had evolved from *how* to *why*. We'd be lying if we didn't admit that backpacking is hard work. The detailed planning takes months. And once we're there, the daily effort of walking up actual mountains with all we need to survive on our backs is no small task. Once at camp, we use up most of lunch's calories just setting up our temporary home. And the evenings get cold, just when we want relief from the elements and a nice hot shower, giving us a temporary reprieve from the effort of the day.

This type of vacationing requires that most of the time the family is spent within a small radius—a blessing and a curse. It's highly concentrated time together—all day, every day. I do miss my alone time and my own personal space complete with air quality that does not include an eleven-year-old's gaseous emissions or foul-smelling feet. But mostly, I recognize that we are spending minutes, days, weeks, and months of time with our children as we watch them grow. With only eighteen years to be together before they will most likely fly the coop, I am so grateful that we have these intense times together, where we literally eat every meal together, walk every step of the day together, see the same sights together. At any moment, we can grab each other's hands and take on the day… together.

All the challenges melted away as the hike from the Bear Creek cutoff trailhead up the Bear Creek drainage basin took us through spectacular, mind-blowing scenery. Not part of the JMT, it was our chosen connector to the famous trail and it truly was, as John Muir coined, "a mirror reflecting the Creator." Slab granite lined the canyon walls with flat pools of water that flowed down to the next part of the flowing stream. We followed the gorgeous waterway the entire uphill climb. Massive granite slabs created eddies and waterfalls with majestic Western Juniper and Lodgepole trees growing out of cracks in the granite. Some of the isolated pools of blue green water seemed to have little cherubs fluttering around in this heavenly setting.

The truth is, most vacations really do take a lot of work to pull off. The goal is always the same: refreshment, clearing of the mind, and a break from the day-to-day tasks we all bear. Immersing ourselves in nature for days on end slowly strips the mind of the millions of inputs it usually has to process and replaces it with singular thinking, usually about what the senses are perceiving.

Northern Carolina State University professor Robin Moore is well known for her research that promotes the vital connection between the environment and children. She writes: "Children live through their senses. Sensory experiences link the child's exterior world with their interior, hidden affective world." [53]

So as I thought on the 'why,' Cade's euphoric smile and cheers as he plunged into Bear Creek came into focus. Outside, the mind is freed up to experience fully. A simple bath awakened his awareness of his senses: the cold shock to the skin, the smell of the nearby pine trees, the sounds of the water rushing over rocks, the taste of the pure mountain stream as it splashed in our mouths, and the feel of the sun as it warmed and dried his body. What is just another thing to do on most other types of vacations or at home becomes the full experience itself. It's fun. It's just plain fun.

And Moore would argue that, "freedom to explore and play with the outdoor environment through the senses in their own space and time is essential for healthy development of an interior life."[51]

One such hiker in search of a healthy interior life explained why he flew all the way from Minnesota to hike in California. "It's real living out here. You're fully alive; it's the real deal."

Or as one entry from a JMT thru-hiker wrote in the VVR log book on July 2nd in 2010: "This is living! Wouldn't want to do it any other way, this is the time and place to be awake, alert, and growing stronger every day. Live on the edge and every day your horizon expands."

And nothing makes one feel more alert or on the edge of an expanding horizon than crossing paths with a bear, except perhaps crossing paths with a mamma bear and her two cubs. While Bekah was characteristically singing as she hiked in the lead position, completely happy, Cory suddenly yelled, "Bekah! Cade! Stop!"

I froze. Looking around I saw the culprit. A brown mama bear was running across the trail, chasing her two little cubs up the tree. We had already "met" this trio the night before when we set up camp at Bear Creek. They had casually strolled past us, keeping a good 500 yards distance. Undoubtedly, this mamma was training her cubs to glean food from the humans who frequent their stomping grounds. They kept their distance that night and with the clean camp we kept, they did not even enter our area.

It wasn't too surprising to meet up with them again, but startling just the same. Most California black bears are pretty harmless, but mamma bears guarding their cubs can be a different story altogether. Once that mamma bear was standing guard under the tree with her adorable young cubs dutifully peering at us from up high, Cory said, "Okay, we can walk now. Go slow."

"Should we take some pictures?" I asked.

"That could be fun. She seems at ease." Cory pulled out his camera, but as he turned toward the mamma, she moved a few feet toward him, prompting a change of mind. "On second thought, let's just go. Remember this one in your mind."

"She sure is comfortable around humans," I noticed.

"Yeah, she's had success getting food from hikers, that's for sure." Cory said.

Onward we went, cooing a little over the cuddly cuteness of her cubs but saddened that they were getting raised with poor habits. Then, less than two hours of encountering the little bear family, a larger black bear came bounding across the trail, headed straight for a sunny meadow. He was completely undisturbed by us and got busy tearing apart a fallen log in search of termites to feast on. Four bears in one morning—that was fully engaging. Staring at a massive, beautiful, and large freely-roaming creature like a 300-pound bear extinguished all other thoughts beside said creature. Fully alive.

In the same morning we experienced two very different bear sightings. Mr. Black Bear was healthy, doing what all good bears do as he scrounged for his feast in snags in a meadow far away from people. He hung out in his natural habitat, oblivious to us pretzel-toting humans, as happy as he could be in his meadow cafe.

Mamma bear, however, was circling Bear Creek the night before, teaching her cubs that people equal food, hoping to nab a bag of Cheetos and share them with her babes. The California Fish and Wildlife department's marketing campaign to save bears reminds people that a "fed bear is a dead bear." Sadly, we enter their world, introduce them to tasty treats like marshmallows and chocolate (what bear could resist that!) and then get nervous about their over friendly proximity to our camps. When they lose their instinctive fear of humans they cross over into targeted animals with euthanasia or relocation as their future.

Keeping a clean camp is all it takes to avoid either ending. Once we witnessed backpackers content to stay in their tent while a hungry bear clawed at the garbage they'd hung in bags on a tree. A year later that bear was euthanized for its repetitive successful hits on campsites. How sad. Bears are successful only when we are negligent. Following food storage regulations from the National Park and Forestry Services can help keep bears out of oatmeal and instead, clawing at dead trees for bugs.

We hiked on. Large bear prints plainly marked the trail all the way to the Sandpiper Lake turnoff. We stayed highly alert, hoping to see more bears in action. At one point, a few prints headed in the opposite direction, making it appear that the bear we tracked had turned around. Within a few feet, though, more tracks appeared facing the direction we were headed.

Chapter 17

An Opportunity To Wonder

Everybody needs beauty as well as bread, places to play in and pray in, where nature may heal and give strength to body and soul alike.

~ John Muir, 1912 [55]

∻⁀⁀∽

Day 13: Sandpiper Lake, layover; 4-mile day hike to upper Sandpiper Basin

My horizon was expanding as we all were experiencing what it meant to feel fully alive and fully engaged. Thankfully, it didn't expand to include a threatening encounter with a bear. In fact, we did not see the bears that left their footprints on the trail again, though their prints and ours mingled as we marched on in the warmth of another glorious summer day. Every step got me closer to an unspoken, yet just as real, goal of the summer. I still had a foot dangling in my other life… the life of comforts without bear paws, emergency help, friends, and email. What was going on back home? I had not yet completely immersed myself in our experience. I could sense that I was getting close, and something finally shifted on the banks of Sandpiper Lake.

Our kids, though, were all in. Both feet. Their remarks said it all.

"Come quick, Cade! It's a toad! It's huge!"

"Holy cow, Mama! Look at the moon!"

These were declarations of wonder over normally overlooked treasures on our journey. Two weeks of watching the sun rise and set made us aware of and become synced with the natural cycles of light and dark. We awoke with the sun and crawled into our tents when it set each evening.

I marveled at how city-dwelling life protects us so much from nature that we usually have no idea what stage the moon is in and where it sits in the night sky. We don't see the toads hopping by or what the local ants are carrying to their nest.

But outdoors, at our campsites, we watched the moon wax each night, getting slightly larger each twenty-four-hour period, casting a blue and white illumination over an otherwise pitch-black land, as bright as sunlight. We watched little ants carry large flies over long distances and even play dead. Yes, we learned that ants can play dead.

Our rhythm had shifted. We no longer talked about, "what we'll do when we get back." Our energy output had adjusted so it was no longer too much work to set up and tear down camp, sitting on the ground to eat had become as comfortable as sitting at a kitchen table, spending the entire day walking had become what the body craved rather than dreaded.

Having never spent more than five nights in a row away from civilization, these feelings were new to me, surprising. I had never really immersed myself long enough to completely feel the clutter of my city-world slip away. Short trips made me feel like a stranger in both worlds. Now I began to feel less like a stranger and more like a friend to this place.

Two days earlier we left Vermillion Valley Ranch and hiked sixteen miles and climbed 3000 ft. We left the JMT highway for an 11,000 foot high mountain lake named Sandpiper, a spectacular basin off the beaten path. Cory just can't resist taking us to seldom-visited paradise locations.

But getting to this point taxed us, as it required boulder hopping over a few miles of cross-country route finding. A mild headache hovered in the background for a few days, triggering those unwanted hidden fears that continued to cower in the shadows. Adjusting to the daily output of calories burnt and sweat produced made it very difficult to eat and drink enough. Our bodies are simply not used to processing gallons of water a day so on the early days of the trip, we drank a lot, and peed a lot but didn't absorb enough. We incorporated coconut water into our hydration regime, which is loaded with five essential electrolytes—sodium, magnesium, calcium, potassium, and phosphorus—to keep our bodies hydrated and help us perform our best. Coconut water also contains as much potassium as a banana, which helps prevent cramping. With the heat on the west side of the range at least fifteen degrees warmer than where we had hiked before, my body wasn't keeping up with the changes, yet, though the coconut water was most definitely helping.

As the pressure on the right side of my head increased over the two days of hiking, so did my anxiety. Fear is one of the barriers that keeps people from getting too deep into a wilderness area. Let's face it, fear has the power to keep us from many things. Its grip is strong and convincing, often guiding our life decisions. And even sixteen years after that notorious day in the Eagle Cap Wilderness, memories still haunted me. Doubts about venturing out as far as we did that summer began to swirl around in my mind.

The contrast between the carefree spirits of my children and my own was stark. This contrast plainly danced in front of me, showing me another possibility, reminding me of how I used to skip along trails without a care in the world. The internal voice replaying the fear tape in my mind was the gatekeeper keeping me from the airy, jaunty, untroubled disposition that characterized my children.

We might think, at first, that getting out on the trail we will teach the kids so much, which is true. But in the end, they will teach us as much, if not more, than we teach them as they embrace their days without baggage and with a child's eye of wonder.

Hiking in lower elevations and staying relatively close to the trailhead is one thing, but as we continued to advance deeper into the wilderness, while I smiled at the kids on this day, inside I could hardly breathe. Granted, we were standing at 10,500 feet, so that could have been a part of the breathlessness, but the truth was, I was terrified. And I was mad at myself for being terrified. All the great moments out here and successful trips were not working to rid me of this gnawing feeling that came and went randomly. Today it decided to strike again. Ultimately, I didn't trust my own body. Would it collapse, unconscious, into a seizure on that trip, on that day, or maybe the next day? If altitude triggered my collapse, could it happen again?

Terrified or not, we were en route, backpacks secured, heading up a trail, surrounded by menacing, dark, and looming peaks. I couldn't just roll up in a ball and refuse to walk. We had already hiked for about fifty miles and our truck was still fifty miles ahead. Two pairs of trusting little eyes looked to me for guidance and confidence. With the wind howling through towering trees dressed in dark shadows, I feigned a weak smile and pressed on, scared.

As I walked I rationalized that sometimes in order to conquer fears, we simply have to do the fearful thing anyway; we just do it scared. How would I ever know if I could do what I had grown to love? I had spent years hiking because I loved it, but always aware of the thread of fear that taunted me whenever it decided to. I was more determined than ever to get to the other side of this wall of anxiety but had no idea how to do that.

I could live a safe life, never any farther from a doctor than a phone call, or I could live life, free. I wanted that. So I walked on. At times, I became completely absorbed in the beauty and the amusement of being with my family. At other times, I was nearly paralyzed with the "what if?" thoughts that pounded my senses.

Finally, I pushed pause on my internal dialogue to look around, viewing some of the most dramatic scenery I had ever witnessed. With 360 degree views of massive granite peaks, multiple lakes, dizzying waterfalls, and vibrant meadows filled with Sierra wildflowers, it was my favorite location so far.

Sometimes in life we have a turning point, a tangible moment in time that permanently changes us. That moment happened for me on the shores of Sandpiper Lake. As I sipped some refreshingly cold glacier water and listened to our kids as they explored the shoreline, I felt myself—for the first time—completely show up on the scene.

I always thought that the breakthrough moment would be ushered in on a great white horse, would sweep me off my feet, and dramatically reunite me with my former, carefree self. The moment wasn't dramatic at all. It was simple. But for all its simplicity, it was real. God Himself seemed to reach inside my mind, grab the tape recorder that was stuck on play, and throw it off the highest cliff, to smash into a million pieces on the canyon floor.

And in its place was this reality: I was at high altitudes and I was conscious! I was beyond conscious; I was vibrantly alive. The sky was a vivid hue of blue, cradling a golden sun that sent rays of light dancing over the water like a thousand sparkling diamonds. The air was cool but with a gentle warm breeze. A few birds sang to the rhythm of the water as it quietly lapped the shoreline. Soaring high above the basin rugged peaks overlooked the majestic landscape with authority.

I sat down on the chilled granite slab feeling the slight burn in my lungs that comes from a good climb and the warmth of the air against my skin when it occurred to me—I need not fear my body any longer. It got me there after all and I felt amazing. If the moment in the Eagle Cap

Wilderness some years earlier defined me as a girl with an unpredictable flaw that could rear up at any moment, than this moment redefined me as a girl who had decided to no longer let that define her. When the heart is convinced, like my heart suddenly was in that moment, then all that's left is for the mind to choose. And my mind was ready to grab ahold of a new definition of self that spoke of life and hope, not death and fear.

Marveling at the night sky speckled with more points of light than my brain could comprehend made my existence seem so insignificant. From the grandeur of this massive creation to the incomprehensible amount of stars in the sky to the tiny ants intricately involved in a sophisticated society below the surface of the earth, came a deep awe. I had been given the privilege and honor to exist at all, to have this opportunity to wonder. I was grateful that God chose to breathe life into me. My thoughts took a full 180 degree turn from fear and insignificance to confidence, courage, and ultimately, significance. As I sat there, totally consumed with both the beauty of what was a gorgeous high mountain lake and the awareness that I was actually there taking it in, a simple, but profound thought flashed in my mind: this is stunning and I am here.

I am.

None of us knows the number of our days. The day I sat there I was 12,706 days old. My fear was wrapped up in a fancy little package that boiled down to this—I wanted to be around for many more days. For years more, really. I like living! More than any other activity we had engaged in, hiking in the wilderness made me face my own mortality and the mortality of my family. The beauty of it was that hanging out on the edge of my comfort zone challenged my unconscious belief systems to become conscious. Once exposed, these beliefs were examined. Were they truth? Were they running my life without me even knowing it?

As top-selling national author Bo Stern stated on her blog, "Only God knows the number of my days and He knows what each day holds. He has plans, not just for my whole life, but for each day of my life. [56]

Fearful of not living to see the next day was robbing me of enjoying the day I had. As I experienced the beauty of Sandpiper Lake, I felt a fifteen-year tyranny on my life lift, because for the first time, the joy in that moment was not sharing the platform with fear. It was standing there alone.

All because I chose to hike—scared. Courage, after all, is not the absence of fear. It's marching forward with fear.

Yes, I am sure fear is one of the barriers that keeps individuals from exploring the wilderness. It threatened, very loudly, to keep me on the city side of a trailhead. The unknown seems unsafe, but pressing into these fears can bring forth victory, freedom, and healing.

John Muir spoke of pain and fear best when he penned these words in his July 20, 1860 journal entry: "No pain here, no dull empty hours, no fear of the past, no fear of the future. These blessed mountains are so compactly filled with God's beauty, no petty personal hope or experience has room to be." [57]

As fear dissipated, I was free to marvel, as John Muir marveled. The beauty of our surroundings was so complete that finally, past fears had no room to be.

Chapter 18

The Courtyard

Drinking this champagne water is pure pleasure, so is breathing the living air, and every movement of limbs is pleasure, while the whole body seems to feel beauty when exposed to it as it feels the camp-fire or sunshine, entering not by the eyes alone, but equally through all one's flesh like radiant heat, making a passionate ecstatic pleasure glow not explainable. One's body then seems homogeneous throughout, sound as a crystal
~ John Muir, July 20, 1860 journal entry [58]

Day 14: Sandpiper Lake to Marie Lake, 4 miles plus a 2-mile trek around Marie Lake

I awoke with an unusual lightness to my spirit. What was mountain living going to feel like without the veil of fear? Was the fear really gone?

Pushing through the previous day's fears allowed us to venture off the JMT to arrive at what became one of our favorite locations of the summer. Somehow hiking where we don't see very many people like we do on the popular JMT had always been so intimidating that I often refused to do it. But this time, I didn't cower. I just said, "OK." It was hard but oh, was it worth it. Sandpiper was a true, glorious, off-the-beaten-path upper basin that few ever see. The kids swam for hours. A spontaneous morning stream hike stretched until lunch, where we all walked in ankle deep water that followed the bubbling stream as it curved and meandered over rocks and small waterfalls. We enjoyed an afternoon of route-finding as we cross-country trekked to the upper lakes of the Sandpiper Basin while the kids asked us to tell them—again— the story of how we met and the years leading up to getting married.

This new release from gripping fear brought me to an internal place I had never experienced before when deep in a wilderness. I could let myself get lost in the retelling of our story, the birth of our family, while taking in the beauty of our surroundings. The afternoon was light hearted; suddenly, we were reliving our early college days and the funny twists and turns of falling in love.

Though I looked the same to my family as we all walked through the basin, I all but floated next to them. It occurred to me how absolutely draining and heavy fear is on our lives; without it, I barely touched the ground.

Once again, John Muir's June 23, 1869, journal entry was inspiring: "Oh, these vast, calm, measureless mountain days, inciting at once to work and rest!" [59]

Had I ever truly rested in the wilderness? How could I have? Rest implies an inner calm that could find the mountain days "measureless." Facing off against fear opened a door that ushered me into a place I had not known. Perhaps over the next few weeks I would find true rest. At that point, I knew only that I had entered an entirely new landscape, one that was both alluring and invigorating.

The next morning we headed to Marie Lake, just a few miles down the trail from Sandpiper Lake. Even that afternoon stroll traversing past quaint coves swarming with Golden Trout and gurgling streams over grassy tarns was somehow more colorful and vibrant than previous landscapes had been. Under the 13,400 foot jagged edged peaks of Mt. Hilgard, Mt. Gabb, and Mt. Abbott, I was deeply present, fully alive, and utterly happy.

Fear that I would collapse at any moment was gone and in its place was joy, peace, harmony, and a quiet soul that slowly took in my surroundings. These feelings were all new. Brand new.

It's not that I had spent every moment of the past fifteen years hiking in gut-wrenching fear, but it sat there, like an impassable wall in the distance, hemming me in. Many days I didn't even notice the wall but some days it stopped me in my tracks. I functioned just fine inside that courtyard. It was a large enough space with nice enough views. Only when I got adventurous, when I got curious and wanted to test myself, try something more challenging, go further, go deeper, go beyond my self-imposed wall, did I get hurt. Every time I slammed into it. And I never argued. I just went back to my courtyard, trapped inside that space, frozen in an eternal winter-like season.

So when I tiptoed out of my winter courtyard, past the wall that had fenced me in, my senses were consumed, first, by the warmth of springtime. I was suddenly aware that the safe and protected wintery world of my courtyard had actually been my jail. Like time-lapsed photography, the landscape changed quickly from winter to spring. I watched huge drifts of snow rapidly melt away, turning into ponds that the sun could now sparkle on. Green hillsides became covered with hundreds of flowers in every imaginable color. I saw blues and reds and pinks and yellows where I had only seen a black and white world. The sky reflected a blue intensity, deeper than I had ever witnessed. And when I looked down at my feet, I suddenly knew why I had felt so light. The heavy balls and chains that shackled them (that I thought everyone carried around which had stopped me from questioning their existence) were gone.

In that June 23rd journal entry, John Muir continued, "Days in whose light everything seems equally divine, opening a thousand windows to show us God."

I was so attracted to his writings because they painted an abandoned appreciation that I couldn't reach, but wanted to. This guru of the mountains could sit on a rock and watch a bird land on a tree limb and appreciate it so deeply that it would become another "window to show [Muir] God." I saw about half of what danced in front of my eyes, while John Muir saw it all.

The promised peace of wilderness travel was speaking to my soul. Through the power and force of nature's marvelous perfection, God communicates to us. And my way of communicating back was to marvel.

When we marvel at and care for His creation, we marvel at and care for God. An important distinction as we marvel is that we do not worship creation—but that instead, creation is pointing us to worship the Creator.

To be in love with all that God created is to be amazed. I began to see the phenomenal, the incredible, in every moment out there—that nothing was to be taken for granted or overlooked. I stood like Bambi on new legs, without the protection of the wall, my courtyard, shaking a little, but so excited to tackle the rest of that trip with my new fresh legs and fresh eyes. What would it feel like to hike these trails with a mind that was not cluttered with thoughts of a looming accident? What would I think about instead? What would I have space in my mind to notice?

Cory and Bekah at Marie Lake, Ansel Adams Wilderness.

Our campsite that night was tucked away from the crowds on a flat granite slab with a perfect grassy ramp that lead to the lake. Six days in a row without a cloud in the sky added more charm to our excursion. Without access to the weather channel, we were unaware of a strong cold front that would bring unusual rain and would follow us for the rest of the summer, creating challenges we were not used to dealing with in the typical sunny climate of the summer Sierras. As a photographer who loves to capture moody skies, these are the storms that Cory lives for.

As we sat at Marie Lake, the gentle breeze and warm sun suggested we had a few days to wait until moody skies might grace the evening. Such awareness was new to me. Weather usually happened on the other side of the window while I went about my business, inside. Now, we were going about our business without windows or walls. So for us, like for Muir, things like the clouds in the sky and the birds soaring over Marie Lake became the main characters in our evening entertainment.

Chapter 19

Find Out

I only went out for a walk, and finally concluded to stay out till
sundown, for going out, I found, was really going in.

~ *John Muir* [60]

⁓⁓⁓

Day 15: Marie Lake to Muir Trail Ranch (MTR); 8 miles,
3000 ft. elevation drop

Our evenings took on a cozy feel as the family quietly
gathered around camp to hear me read from the *No. 1 Ladies
Detective Agency* by Alexander McCall Smith a delightful and
clever read, set in Botswana. We learned a bit about Africa as
we traversed our own wild American lands. Then, as soon as
we snuggled into our tents, Cory, both fearless trail guide and
deeply engaged dad, read the entertaining and heartwarming
stories of James Herriot, the country vet of Darrowby, in *All
Creatures Great and Small.* Even after a day of route
planning, map following, water purifying, and meal

preparing, Cory still had energy to read to the family. Entertaining us right into blissful slumber.

These kinds of traditions, when weaved into trail time, made it so much more fun for the whole family. We finished book number 1 on the tails of Mma Ramotswe of the *No. 1 Ladies' Detective Agency.* As we descended down from Selden Pass into Muir Trail Ranch, we looked forward to meeting up with Mma Ramotswe again, as she waited in our resupply bucket in the form of book number 2.

Within minutes of opening the wooden gate at Muir Trail Ranch, we met Dan, a high-energy dad of a nine- and thirteen-year-old who worked at the ranch in between his shifts as a Fresno firefighter. His enthusiasm over seeing kids passing through the ranch was exactly what our tired kids needed. He bent down and looked Bekah right in the eye and asked her, "Did you hike all the way here? I am so impressed!"

Then he saw Cade hanging in the wings and ran over to him, "And how old are you, buddy?"

When he turned his attention to us, I could see sincere amazement in his eyes. "I never see kids coming through this ranch. I'd love to get mine out here but they just get tired and end up not liking it. How do you do it?"

He whipped out his phone and took a picture of our two kids to attempt to inspire his own to try it again. It wasn't the first time a hiker had done this. I began to wonder if sighting a kid on the trail was more rare than the elusive cougar.

Later that night, John, a dad in his thirties, appeared on the ledge right below our granite perch for the night. We called down to him with a friendly hello, which he returned with, "Are you the folks who are hiking 200 miles this summer with your kids?" He came to get tips, wondering how he could motivate his nine- and twelve-year-old boys to hike with him. His eleven- and sixteen-year-old boys loved it, but the other two were not interested.

It would take more conversations with folks and more trail time for me to process it all so that I could formulate an answer to the question that we received on a daily basis. The truth was, for the entire summer, we had not seen a single hiker under the age of fourteen and we only encountered a handful of teenagers. For every parent we passed asking us how we were pulling this off, we realized hundreds more were asking (or maybe had stopped asking) whom we'd never meet.

We hiked on in slow pursuit of a better answer for these parents. How *did* we get our kids to hike?

Chapter 20

The Why

We need the tonic of wilderness.
~Henry David Thoreau

❧

Day 16: MTR to Franklin Meadow; 8 miles, 1000 ft. of climbing

The next morning, as these conversations swirled around in my mind, we picked up our three buckets of food at Muir Trail Ranch where I met Rick, a Pacific Crest Trail (PCT) hiker. Assuming I worked for the ranch, he approached me and asked if I had pliers to fix his broken hiking pole.

"Oh, no. I'm just another hiker like you. I don't work here," I explained.

Over the next ten minutes I heard of his trail trials that included a broken water pump, then a broken stove, and finally two bouts of Giardia, all within the miles between Mexico and where he stood that day. A few more questions from me spurred him to reveal why, despite such difficulties, he was compelled to press on hiking the Mexico to California section of the PCT. He needed to refocus and find himself after recently losing his mom to a swift acting stomach cancer. His plan was to take as long as it took to get to Oregon's southern border.

It Had already occurred to me that the question of "how" we got our kids out in the backcountry was deeply imbedded in the bigger question of "why?" So why hike 200 plus miles every summer with our kids?

Young hikers are reluctant because they are not internally motivated. They have not figured out that the excitement on a backpacking trip comes quietly in the whispers of the trees and the warmth of the sunrise, in the comfort as dreams unfold during long talks to pass the trail miles away, in the smiles around another delicious camp dinner that end caps a day full of successful effort.

They haven't realized that the solidarity of holing up with a video game is trumped by the community one joins as their hiking group makes its way—step by step—to its destination. That which cannot be googled is not worthy of their time. They haven't grasped the why.

As parents we can help our children grasp the why by letting them experience nature from a young age. Since our kids were born, we haven't missed a summer of backpacking with them. It would have been much easier to leave them at home than to tackle the monumental task of figuring out how to take them with us. But early on we chose to include them, which gave them the chance to figure out the why on their own. They have no way of doing that sitting at home.

They have to be out, to figure it out.

With over twenty-five years of backpacking experience and ten years as a boys camp wilderness guide and camp counselor in the Sierra mountains, Cory has made it his mission to become an expert on the *how*, especially when it comes to exposing kids to the wilderness. He was passionate to learn the *how* because he had experienced the *why* countless times as he witnessed the transformation of literally hundreds of inner city Los Angeles boys challenged to become men through the life-changing two weeks they spent at Pyles Boys Camp.

Some of the best years Cory had growing up were in the Golden Trout Wilderness at Pyle's camp in a stunning section of the southern Sierras. It was here that he fell in love with wilderness and watched as experiences in its rugged grandeur changed the course of young boys' lives forever and ultimately, his own life as well.

These were the boys on the fence. Often they were losing hope for their lives. In the amazing resilience that children have, though, they hadn't given up completely.

Seven days were spent in camp doing everything from ropes courses to horseback riding, building unity among the groups and confidence within the kids. The real transformations, though, happened when the kids, fitted with backpacks stuffed with gear, hit the trail with their group of seven other new friends and their counselor/wilderness guide for a week.

Coming from Los Angeles, Bakersfield, Orange County, and other surrounding areas, these boys had rarely ventured out of their smog-filled cities. But at camp they were completely removed from the streets they were used to and suddenly had to depend on each other and themselves in ways they never had to before. They felt new fears they had to overcome as they looked out into the dark forest at night.

The girth of the trees, the height of the mountains, the speed of the rushing rivers awed these city dwelling kids. The quiet of the forest contrasted sharply with the chaos of the city, the chaos of their lives, which they no longer had to fight through each minute of their day to survive. At Pyles, they could breathe deeply and rediscover their "inner" kid.

Joseph, from Los Angeles, reflected on his time at camp. "Pyles Camp opened a door in my life that has inspired me to become a better person by allowing me to experience things I was not sure I would ever get the chance to experience. I have experienced the unforgettable."

We are all deeply affected by the stability, beauty, and grandeur of a natural place. It is, as Joseph said, "unforgettable." Incoming research continues to support the strategy of using outdoor settings to teach youth, while strategies to reach kids that keep them in their same environment often fall short. Why?

A man loved by many, simply known by his camp name, Rocky, was Pyles Boys Camp Director in 1997. He reflected on why it can be so difficult to reach at-risk youth in their camp newsletter: "Because often they have no hope. No hope for a better life, no hope for a family, no hope for a job and a future. Kids caught up in the gang lifestyle often do not see a future for themselves. There is no concern if they or others live or die. If there is no hope, there is then no concern for the present or the future. This concept is often overlooked in working with at-risk youth. But it is important. Before there can be *any* change, before any jobs training or rehabilitation program can work, each youth must begin to have hope. They must begin to believe there is a positive future in their lives. I believe this is one of the reasons that Pyles Camp is so effective. Pyles Camp provides an atmosphere of hope. We tell them they are important, that they have value. Our activities build self-confidence and pride. As they begin to accomplish the challenges before them, as they begin to feel the warmth of success, hope grows. And from a base of hope, change can now begin." [61]

When at-risk youth are taken out of their comfort zones, they face the unknown, new challenges, and experience new fears. They might have street smarts, but none of them have trail smarts. They are all equalized in the wilderness, where rankings in their gangs gain them nothing on the trail. Unlike gang life, through daily goals and achievements in camp, these boys, sometimes for the first time in their lives, get to feel success. They don't have to wait four years to feel success in the event that they somehow pull off graduating from school. The high they get from this new sense of accomplishment is a powerful shaper of who they become when they head back to the city.

The beauty around them is a gift to their senses as it contrasts with the smog, sirens, and overcrowded cities they come from. It gently points toward a calmer spirit, reminding them that there is a life outside their trials that is good and beautiful and worth living for.

Building into kids early the value and reasons to get outside ignites a passion for the "why" of doing it at all. It gives them more tools in their personal toolkit for life. Tyson, a thirteen-year-old Pyles Boys camper, left camp with a gift from the mountains that allowed him to realize for the first time in his life that, "My life counts! And I can do it!" The Tysons of the world give us a glimpse into the transformative power of outdoor experiences. It gives even more reason to work so hard to include our children when we head to the mountains, forests, and rivers of our beautiful planet because of the undeniable truth that kids thrive when exposed to nature.

Conversations with John, Rick, and Dan made it crystal clear to me that we must grab a hold of the *why*, like young Tyson did, in a place that's deep in our hearts. This way, when our poles and stoves break (and two of the four poles we brought failed), we get Giardia, or simply have a physically challenging day on the trail, we continue on, because we want to continue on. Our hearts won't give us a choice.

Of course, knowing the "how" can help reduce the chances of broken gear and lethargy, but without the why, the how will never matter.

The *why* propelled us out of MTR at the low elevation of 7,500 ft with our heaviest packs yet, stuffed with six days of food. We spent the entire day walking uphill in mid-80 degree heat. Despite the heavy packs, the hike was the kind of beauty that could convince anyone to join us. We hiked along the San Joaquin River Valley with the river raging through granite slabs and boulders as our constant companion, urging us on.

I held my breath as I watched our kids pass over a few exposed areas. One slip could mean sure death, plunging 100 ft. down into a raging river. But they did great, like pros. The warm walk up the valley ended for us before a bridge that crossed the river. We spent the night in Franklin Meadow, our campsite nestled in the trees next to a gentle flowing section of the San Joaquin River.

Cade could hardly wait to test out his new fishing pole that he'd made out of a willow branch. It had stuck out of his backpack like a TV antenna for the previous seventeen miles, sporting a fly that a generous JMT thru-hiker at Muir Trail Ranch had given him. One of Cade's many charming attributes is his intense focus when something grabs ahold of him. When he is inspired, he can think of nothing else and will devote every waking minute to perfecting his skills and learning about that which has inspired him. Without anything other than letting him walk in the woods past rivers and streams that housed thousands of trout, Cade became fixated on figuring out how to catch them.

I have yet to see Cade get deeply inspired from a screen. It passes the time and like all boys, he is drawn to the flashing lights, but actual unquenchable inspiration that ignites a bottomless fervor can only come from engaging, first hand, with one's world.

Frank Wilson, professor of neurology at the Stanford University School of Medicine concurs. "We've been sold a bill of goods—especially parents—about how valuable computer-based experience is. We are creatures identified by what we do with our hands."

Richard Louv adds, "Much of our learning comes from doing, from making, from feeling with our hands, and though many would like to believe otherwise, the world is not entirely available from a keyboard." [62]

For Wilson, teaching medical students the connection between the heart and a mechanical pump has become tough to do, "because these students have so little real-world experience; they've never siphoned anything, never fixed a car, never worked on a fuel pump, may not even have hooked up a garden hose. For a whole generation of kids, direct experiences in the backyard, in the tool shed, in the fields and woods, has been replaced by indirect learning, through machines. These young people are smart, they grew up with computers, they were supposed to be superior—but now we know that something's missing." [63]

Cade came up with a dream. (I want to catch fish!) He created a plan. He chatted with other fishing connoisseurs and got more excited, more information, and a few needed flies. He hiked for seventeen miles, uphill (both directions, as they say), thinking of nothing else besides how he would outsmart the fish that innocently waited for him. He spent hours crawling through lakeside brush, stalking his fish (for they indeed were his fish), coming up empty. Ankle deep, followed by his adoring sister, our little fisherman ventured into a different section of the river. He refused to give up. Within ten minutes, to our surprise, his homemade pole was bobbing with a six-inch Golden Trout. Cheers echoed off the canyon walls. He caught one more fish that night and went to bed beaming, a blinding glow I'd never seen from him spending time in front of a computer.

When he recounted his favorite moments from our 200-mile trek, without missing a beat, he said, "Making my own fishing pole out of a willow twig," adding with a huge smile, "and it worked! I caught fish with it!"

The *why* just embedded deeper into one eleven-year-old boy's heart.

Cade and Bekah on the JMT.

Chapter 21

New Identities

No synonym for God is so perfect as Beauty. Whether as seen carving the lines of the mountains with glaciers, or gathering matter into stars, or planning the movements of water, or gardening - still all is Beauty!
~ John Muir [64]

❧

Day 17: Franklin Meadows to Evolution Basin; 8 mi, 2000 ft. elevation climb

Anticipation built all day as the highly acclaimed Evolution Basin was within our reach. A day's hike and over 2000 feet of climbing through two more hanging valleys of expansive meadows was all that was between us and one of our favorite basins on the planet. We climbed fast and steady, often catching up to other adult groups making their way.

Stopping at a massive granite slab, I asked, "So what's for lunch, Sergeant O?"

His characteristic raise of one eyebrow accompanied an amused smirk. "I don't know, Yerba Mama. What do you want for lunch?"

Cade and Bekah's eyes darted from "Sergeant O" to "Yerba Mama" trying to make sense of the conversation. The veritable captain and brains behind our hiking expedition naturally led to my spontaneous new nickname of Cory as the Sergeant. To which he quipped a new name for me based on my Yerba Mate addictions in the morning. My mate mornings were my happiest mornings. If I ever skipped the mate, the family knew.

Laughter died down and the dehydrated hummus and chips, sausage, and Oreos became our new focus. Food had a way of doing that with a band of hungry hikers.

Mid-lunch, as I eyed my Oreos waiting patiently for me, I suddenly exclaimed, "We should be the OReOs! The ORegon O'Neills."

Without trying too hard, our new identities on the trail were forming. Temporarily leaving our city lives meant we could leave our former selves with our truck, parked at the trailhead. We could redefine ourselves on the trail—symbolized by new trail names and liberated to-do lists. I found freedom as I turned in my working-mom-with-way-too-much-on-my-calendar persona for my new persona: trail sojourner.

Cory delighted in this as well. When asked what he did for a living, he more often responded with, "I'm a photographer," than "I'm a high school teacher." New trail names completed our rite of passage in our transformation into wilderness wanderers.

As we hiked along after lunch, Cade and Bekah were eager to be renamed as well. Watching her pink sun bonnet bob up and down while she cruised up the trail, we all agreed that she was now Pink Bolt. She kept up with the family in happy cadence.

Our boy needed his manly trail name, too. Chewing up the trail in record style, Cade did everything quickly. He jumped off boulders in camp and set the pace during the day. He became Lightning Feet.

"We need a family cheer!" Bekah offered. "Here, after I say your name, repeat it and when we are done, we'll all say 'Oreos'! Ready? Bekah… Pink Bolt. Cade… "

"Lightning Feet," chimed Cade.

"Momma," she continued.

"Yerba Mama," I responded.

"Daddy!" she said with pride.

Cory concluded the role call with his response, exaggerating the pronunciation as he hung on the a, "Saaaaaargent O!"

Then with one, unified voice we did as instructed by our young girl and all said, after a count of three, "Oreos!" Smiles and giggles were exchanged. We had a family cheer with new names. We shared the JMT with thousands, but this little jingle was just ours, our own unique mark. We used this cheer during the rest of our journey to bind us together and encourage us on our trek, and usually our youngest, Pink Blur, started the cheer.

Trail Entertainment

Rallying cheers and trail songs made for easy miles. If the ants can march up the mountain, then singing about their march just adds charm to ours. As Lightning Feet and I took the lead, Pink Blur and her daddy began to see how long they could keep the marching song going—only limited by fun new words that could rhyme with the next number. The Marching Ants song is one of her favorites, as she most likely related with the "littlest one" that is always stopping to pick up sticks, or climb a tree, or shut the door right before they all go marching down, to the ground, to get out of the rain. Boom! Boom! Boom!

As our littlest one, we were often waiting for Pink Blur to finish packing her pack, put on her shoes, or finish her meal. "Hurry up, Bekah!" was a daily prod. Her sweet daddy usually took it upon himself to hang behind with her on the trail, chatting with her, singing with her, and encouraging her onward. He was the most fit of all of us and could chew up the miles in half the time it took to bring his family with him. But true to Cory's essence, he was there to experience the wilderness with us. Not just to experience the wilderness. Nevertheless, whenever we packed up camp, ate lunch, or got water, we often had to prod Bekah from rest to movement.

On that particular day a small voice inside my heart reared up this warning: "Say that enough and one day you'll turn around and she will have hurried up and grown up."

Whoa. That sobering thought had the right effect. We started noticing what she did do, as clearly, putting on her shoes often didn't make the list. She did a lot of singing. She did a lot of skipping. She did a lot of sitting, looking around, often looking intently at something crawling in the dirt. She did a lot of watching. Mesmerized by trees swaying and birds flying, she could sit (and not put on her shoes) for a half hour or more.

"Hurry up, Bekah!" was the push that brought her back to reality. "Oh, it's pretty cool here but it's not the end. We have to move on, again."

I became curious; if we didn't hurry our littlest, when would she break away on her own? It was if she were giving her surroundings a big hug. I tend to be the first one to break a hug. Maybe I don't want to know how long or short the other person is in it for, so I pull away first. This way, I'll never have to know. I wondered if we didn't pull her out of her hug of the sights she was taking in, when would she choose to pull away? The song played again in my mind, "The littlest stops to tie her shoe… to climb a tree… to dance a jig… to gaze in awe… "

Thank you, littlest one, for joining us out there and for slowing down enough to take note, to ponder, to wonder, and to teach us to do the same. When we can, we will try to give room in our day to let you hug until *you* want to let go.

Pink Blur often took in her day with few words and a content heart. In contrast, Lightning Feet loved to spend miles on the trail dreaming and talking of the latest thing he was building that he'd left behind. Thankfully, he liked to chatter the miles away, because I much preferred listening and thinking over talking. Many trail miles were spent planning, designing, and creating the perfect dream fort that he'd build with Bekah upon our return. He spoke of plans for doors, windows, chairs, tables, and entryway signs. When he wasn't building his future fort, he was designing his mountain bike trail around our property.

Miles on the trail flew by especially quickly when Lightning Feet and Pink Blur hiked together; Lightning Feet relayed every sentence he could remember of the entire Harry Potter series to his sister. I was never more thankful for the lengthiness of these books than I was on the trail. Like a daily feature film, for at least a week, our boy broadcast every detail of the story to his captive audience who enjoyed every second of his retelling. So captivated by the story, she made record time, nearly forgetting the amount of energy she was expending to cover the miles. She hiked fast, keeping up with her mesmerizing storyteller.

And we often hiked in silence. Silence meant the mind finally had its chance to spin and weave tales of its own. Out of these silences often came new strategies for catching trout at our next campsite or memories of some fun moment that happened months earlier. Or sometimes, nothing at all. Without the requirement to multi-task, letting the mind wander was a completely sufficient use of an entire afternoon.

During these quieter moments we took in the magnificence of all that we walked through—ultimately connecting us to the thousands of people who have passed through this very way, seeing this same beauty, this landscape, these glacier carved ridges—which have remained relatively untouched. Residents have come and gone, the economy has surged and plummeted, nations have prospered and perished, and through it all, these mountains have remained, unfazed by human stressors.

Walking on the trail on that most glorious, blue sky day, I was utterly humbled. The grandeur would outlast my lifetime. Experiencing a world that was far larger than ourselves was humbling for kids as well. The soaring glaciers were such a striking contrast to the gloom of the national headlines.

Lightning Feet could think of nothing other than the beautiful, elusive trout he imagined were swimming in streams by the hundreds, unsuspectingly waiting for his fly. The kids couldn't wait to tease the fish with their newly made willow rods.

Cory watched the continuing build-up of the clouds and dreamt of the light show that was sure to happen in the sky over his cherished basin. And I truly enjoyed just the act of moving, all day, through a trail that wound through delightful forests, near glistening lakes, and under massive granite peaks. Camp held for me a place to journal about it all as I attempted to capture this experience that seemed as elusive to corral onto paper as the trout were onto Lightning Feet's hook.

At last, we arrived into the glorious Evolution Basin. Hiking Evolution Basin and Evolution Valley gave us the contrasting landscapes of majestic forests found below 10,000 feet and the near mystical High Sierra dominated by towering peaks of granite, wide blue lakes, and open vistas. It is considered to be one of the most beautiful places in the world. After two days of forest hiking near a river, entering the basin was a shock to the eyes. We traded in the closed-in feeling that comes from walking among giant trees for a wide open basin of granite peaks reaching over 13,000 feet, soaring over the enchanting and expansive Evolution Lake. Our first evening did not fail to deliver. A pink glow illuminated the craggy peaks as the sun set, with Cory happily stationed near the outflow of the lake, capturing the red and yellow sky as it reflected on the water that cascaded over the cliff.

The kids were both calf deep in the outflow of Evolution Lake, patiently stalking their prized prey—the Golden Trout —completely absorbed in their new trail personas.

The beauty of the golden glow over the lake under the radiant orange and yellow sunset fed my soul, inspiring me to exist out there naturally, and not fight against it. Without the veil of fear, I was free to do what I needed to do.

So I did all that I could do: I noticed it. We all noticed it. And then we enjoyed it, together.

Cade and Bekah fishing on Evolution Lake,
Kings Canyon National Park.

Chapter 22

Learning From Fish ('cause who else is out here?!)

I rolled up some bread and tea in a pair of blankets with some sugar and a tin cup and set off... feeding on God's abounding, inexhaustible spiritual beauty bread.
~ John Muir's Menu [65]

~>⌒<~

Day 18: A rest day at Evolution Basin

Cade and Bekah's creative, red-cheeked vibrancy was energizing to be around. Their curiosity propelled them around the next switchback and fostered mornings like this—chasing trout with a willow branch and fishing line until it was too warm for the fish to surface. Observing kids fueled by organic green drinks and veggie packed dehydrated dinners, I became convinced that nutrition on the trail is paramount.

Jim, the owner of VVR, showed me some packaged Honey Bun donut-like pastries that he said JMT thru-hikers buy up like crazy. "See here," he said, pointing to the back of the package, "each one has 580 calories and hikers love the bulk calories in a small package."

I suppose that was one way to do it; cheaper for sure, but did it work? Between the gallons of pure mountain water flushing through our bodies and the perfectly clean air surging through our lungs as the days on the trail added up, I felt my own body get stronger and heal any of the maladies that had built up during the rest of the year. We wanted to aid our bodies restoration with vitamin-packed food and not hinder the process by feeding them chemically laden, corn syrup sweetened calories. After all, we were asking them to hike 200 plus miles.

The quick sugar energy might feel good in the beginning, but the inevitable crash is sure to happen—just as the body needs to surge up a steep hill. It might seem like a good idea to bribe kids up the mountain with sugary treats, but we have found that moods and energy levels stay more consistent with a protein rich, dried fruit/nut, and veggie arsenal. A fun treat of Oreos might endcap a lunch, but it does not string the day together.

People define health in so many ways. Some are satisfied if they don't have a cold, considering that the mark of health. I like how Kris Carr defines health in her book, *Crazy, Sexy Diet*. "Health is more than just the absence of disease. It is the presence of vitality." [66] Vitality brought about by using the organic produce section of the supermarket as our medicine is an addictive way to live. Filling our bodies with power packed, whole food nutrition is complicated, as it's tough to break old habits. It can be challenging to do in these fast-paced, sugar powered times. Challenging, but not impossible.

According to the World Health Organization, 1.6 billion adults and 400 million children worldwide are considered obese. [67] In the United States, the number one killer is heart disease and 80 percent of premature heart attacks and strokes are preventable through lifestyle and diet changes. [68] A combination of eliminating foods with ingredients in them that we can't pronounce and replacing our intake with luscious, gorgeous alkaline veggies and fruits will detoxify our bodies and feed us at a deep cellular level. Check out the appendix at the end of this book for more thoughts about eating on the trail, including recipes.

During the morning as the kids fished, Cade suddenly popped away from the shoreline and bounded over to us, "Would the fish like a grasshopper on my hook instead of this plastic fly?"

"Oh, yeah. They love that!" we said.

That is all it took for both kids to lay their poles aside and set off on a grasshopper hunt. In no time at all, desperate grasshoppers hung on their lines, tempting the wise fish that swam below.

"Daddy, my grasshopper died!" wailed Bekah.

"Oh, Bekah, you can never catch a fish with a dead grasshopper."

So off she went to get a new, fresh, happy bug.

We should take advice from these thriving Golden Trout as we plan our meals out here, choosing food that is alive with enzymes, nutrients, and minerals. If dead, lifeless food isn't good enough for the Golden Trout, then it's probably not good enough for us either.

To Cade's dismay, we later met a professor of biology who had a completely different take on stocking Sierra lakes with Golden and Brown Trout. Not being part of the natural habitat, the trout disrupted the lake's nightlife. They ate the evening bug hatches meant for the tadpoles, frogs, and amphibians that hopped around the shores. No bugs meant no frogs. As we talked to the biologist, we thought back to these toad- and frog-less lakes that were brimming with fish and wondered what the solution might be.

"Frogs have been on a decline across the planet for over twenty years," he explained. "A fungus is killing them off, but a secondary problem are these stocked lakes full of trout that shouldn't be there, tipping the delicate balance of the lake's ecosystem. There is talk of discontinuing lake stocking, at least for the higher elevation lakes."

This did not make Cade happy. And with all the hikers we passed who were sporting fishing rods, I wondered if such policies would curtail the number of hikers to these amazing places. Fewer visitors to these wild lands decreases the numbers of people who fall in love with these same destinations. Were the misplaced Trout really the ones to blame? Would such a drastic policy also reduce the number of advocates who push for policies of protection to these same places?

That night we ate a delicious rehydrated African peanut stew of sweet potatoes mingled with kale and peanut butter. It seemed to give us a second wind, prompting an after dinner hike. The four of us scrambled to a high perch and sat atop boulders gazing out over the glorious Evolution Basin as it sported an angry and promising sky. Things had indeed lined up nicely for Cory's photo shoot. The clouds had been building for a few days and Cory couldn't believe our perfect timing. To be at his favorite basin with an exciting night sky only meant one thing: his perfect photo was almost in the bag.

As if we were waiting for a parade to start, we sat frozen in anticipation as the clouds moved and churned, swirling their dark and light arms across the sky, promising a show we'd never forget. It seemed like a guarantee. Dark clouds boiled and swirled with occasional sun breaks. A magnificent moody sunset was bound to explode over Evolution Basin. Or so we imagined.

Chapter 23

Perfect Timing Redefined

The air was perfectly delicious, sweet enough for the breath of angels, every draught of it gave a separate and distinct piece of pleasure.
~ *John Muir, Letter to Jeanne C. Carr, 1868* [69]

❧

Day 19: Evolution Basin to Sapphire Lake, 3 easy miles; 3-hour day hike to Sapphire Lake high basin

As the evening brought in more wind and dark clouds gathered up for the evening show, the sky melted into a palette of greys and whites. The brilliant pinks, reds, purples, and oranges were not going to join the show that night after all. Instead, the sun's glow danced behind a dark veil of clouds, hiding the light breakthroughs that provide for fiery skies.

With our focus on the massive peaks surrounding the lake to the southwest, we were missing the gentler show happening down the valley in the northwest. Realizing the mountains would remain in darkness, Cory turned around to discover a subdued, yet beautiful, scene playing out behind us. The sun strained through the clouds, creating dramatic crepuscular rays, or "God rays" that reached through a light fog all the way to the earth. Mellow hues of lush green meadows, large pine trees, and soft curving ponds lit up for a few minutes from the long fingers of heaven reaching down to illuminate this cultivated garden-like scene.

We came for a firework show and got a quiet date at a quaint café instead. Two minutes of sun rays straining through the clouds to touch the earth sent a reverent hush over our small crowd.

We came for one thing but were stopped in our tracks in awe over another. The key was letting go of our focus—what we thought was the prize—to see the gift of the evening that was something entirely different, yet spectacular just the same.

Paraphrasing Henry David Thoreau's *Walden*, Michael Baughman writes, "Many men go fishing all of their lives without knowing that it is not fish they are after." [70]

As we progressed through the remainder of the trip, I attempted to look deeper, with my eyes and heart, for what we were really after. I wanted to take my gaze off of the obvious and turn around, where I was sure I could find some God-ray moments and lessons. Unbeknownst to me, my first ray would be discovered later that very evening.

At the first clap of thunder, we scrambled down from our perch to find shelter in our tents. The storm blew in and the sky lit up with flashes that produced deafening thunderous cracks lasting for thirty seconds as the initial blast echoed and rumbled through the deep canyons. Torrential sheets of rain fell, pounding the ground and tents with resounding fury.

Through Cade's excitement and cheers as he witnessed this magnificent display of power we heard Bekah cry, her sweet voice cutting through the pounding rain, "Daddy, I'm scared!"

It's one thing to experience a thunderstorm in a house, but it's a complete sensory overloading, somewhat terrifying experience to endure such a storm in a tent, especially if you're nine.

As the sky flashed and the rumbling surrounded and vibrated our only shelter, our little girl's cries from her tent became more desperate. "Daddy! I'm so scared!"

We calculated a plan for her to sprint to our tent, timed to avoid getting too much water in each tent as we unzipped the doors. Once inside, she sank into the covers between us, with just her pretty blue eyes peering out over the covers and her knuckles white from gripping her sleeping bag so tightly. Within seconds, her fears melted away and in its place were the grins and kisses of a very grateful girl.

The storm raged on but she was no longer alone (or just with her brother) and suddenly, the storm didn't seem so big. Perhaps that is one of the deeper lessons we will take with us when we leave the trail. Obviously, the main event, the main focus, was going out there to see beauty in creation beyond anything imaginable, but perhaps taking a moment to turn around and look at "God rays" shining strong, the message really is: spending every moment together, patiently walking miles of trail together, reinforces to all four of us that together we are in this thing called life.

The repetitive, daily, physical act of walking—together—embeds this truth deeply in the souls of our two kids: in this, and in life, even when the mountain gets steep and the storms violent, we are here for them, with them. They are not alone. They are intricately bound to our family. They can get in our tent and snuggle in close and we'll face the storm together, and in the end, it'll be okay.

So as the sky lit up and the earth trembled, our little girl relaxed and fell asleep, completely oblivious to the storm that raged around us.

On a night we thought Cory was sure to capture a stunning shot we'd never forget, we instead shared a night that would be remembered for a completely different reason.

Lessons of the heart last even longer than a great photo shoot for they become part of who we are, the very fabric that defines us.

Chapter 24

Shavasana

I have reveled and luxuriated amid its plants and mountains
nearly four months. I am well again, I came to life in the cool
winds and crystal waters of the mountains.
~ John Muir, Letter to Jeanne C. Carr, 1868 [71]

Day 20: Sapphire Lake to Dusy Basin; 15 miles, 8000 ft.
elevation change

I stood, baffled by what I stumbled upon—a two-inch
footprint with four or five skinny claws clearly embedded in
the granite rock. There were three other prints, with various
parts smudged, showing the walking path of a small animal.

My first thought was, "some animal must have run over
the poured cement before it set…" and then I stopped short
and realized I might be staring at ancient history. For this was
no cement slab I was standing on; I was on a granite rock,
and those were footprints of an animal I did not recognize,
from a time long ago.

But like so much of what is seen and experienced out here, there is no way to capture fully the sights, sounds, smells, and essence of what it is to be immersed in the wilderness. We attempt through photos and journals to take a piece of the Sierras with us, but its elusive capture is why we feel compelled to do the only thing we can do—return and return often.

Treated as royalty by the Sierra landscape, we slept on a carpet of grass behind a huge slab of granite under the cathedral peak, Mt. Huxley. On the opposite side of the lake from the JMT, we were isolated from the many groups surrounding the lake, and we were protected from the wind.

The power to create this phenomenal world without the interference of man's hand is prominently displayed in the very existence of a towering tree, a singular flower, or a raging river, not to mention the intricate ecosystem that keeps it all functioning. The act, for us, of walking through this sacred land is a continual form of worship to the very Creator who made this all possible. As John Muir drifted enchanted through the Sierras, he reasoned that such grandeur must have a Master Creator, as such magnificence opens, "a thousand windows to show us God."

We woke up, like we do every morning, ready for another day. As the first birds started to sing and the sun made itself known, we didn't really know if it would be one of those rare days that stands out from all the rest or if it would fade into the blur that creates our past. This day, as it turned out, was the former.

We challenged ourselves with a fifteen-mile goal. If we could climb Muir Pass, head seven miles down Leconte

Canyon and then climb 3000 ft up into Dusy Basin, we'd knock an entire night off our trip. It would take all day to realize this goal. Then we'd head out from Dusy Basin to South Lake where Nana and Papa would be waiting to shuttle us to our truck so we could enjoy a few days of camping with them and resupply and continue on for sixty more miles to our final destination.

Accomplishing a fifteen-mile day of climbing over one pass at nearly 12,000 feet, descending down to 7,500 feet and then back up to camp in Dusy Basin, which sits around 11,000 feet, would make for our most challenging day yet. Could we actually pull this off?

Our kids started the day with a quiet determination in their eyes, but that determination came with its nefarious partner: doubt.

I think back to the time leading up to the first day; the subtle ways eyes darted and shoulders slumped spoke of the quiet demon of doubt that swirled beneath the excitement. There might have been fear that they'd be the one who'd "fail" the family and stop the trip short.

To make it to our destination in time to set up camp and make dinner, we knew we had to get up early and break camp quickly to be hiking by 8 a.m. Our two determined kids woke up with a fire lit under them, ate fast, and did their necessary chores to meet goal number one: we touched trail at 8 a.m. We were just in time to watch a group of retired old men in their birthday suits enjoying a morning plunge in Sapphire lake. They were clearly in their element and didn't so much as look up to wave good morning. We could hear them laughing and quipping one liners back and forth the entire ascent up the trail towards Muir Pass.

I could sense a nervous, excited energy in our troops as we began the ascent to Muir Pass. Normally, the wilderness is devoid of all man-made comforts, but the top of Muir Pass is an exception. Sitting atop the pass is a spectacular, circular rock hut built in 1931 by the Sierra Club. As we sat in it on that blue sky, chilly August day, it was hard to imagine how many have been kept alive in the shelter waiting out blizzards and wind storms, sometimes holing up for a week until it was safe to move on.

With that pass under our belts, we began the descent to the bottom of LeConte Canyon. We had to make it to the junction of the JMT and the trail that would take us up to Dusy Basin by 2:30 if we wanted to accomplish this. Resupplying out of the South Lake Trailhead added an extra twenty-seven miles of hiking, but for us was well worth it as Dusy Basin is one of our favorites and makes for stunning photography. This outer edge of Kings Canyon National park is a gold mine of photographic opportunities.

Our determined duo strategized that we'd need to eat a thirty-minute lunch to stay on schedule. The steep downhill followed the San Joaquin River, which ran alongside the rugged 13 and 14, 000 ft Leconte Divide. It is a stunning canyon to traverse with hanging meadows full of delightful tarns and green grass. Flowers lined our path. To Cory, this section of trail is what Heaven must look like. However, heavenly and rugged do not equate to easy lunch spots. Right about the time we were ready to just lunch in the middle of the trail, a flat spot opened up, convenient and safe for accessing the river for water refills.

"Isosceles Peak" by Cory O'Neill, Kings Canyon National Park.

We eventually realized that we were lunching near the infamous granite monster formed by two giant boulders wedged together to form it's mouth. Carefully placed boulders create its eyes and well placed pointed rocks form its teeth. All who lunch here must take a few shots inside the mouth, proving to all that they survived the granite monster of the JMT.

Also taking advantage of the unique spot was a group of four, with whom we shared conversation of the joys of the JMT. The lively conversations and photo shoots caused our thirty-minute lunch to stretch into a long hour and the kids feared we'd lost our chance at the fifteen-mile day accomplishment.

With our kids more determined than ever, we headed on, our sites set on that junction. Fast hiking and trail games

"Granite Monster" rock, Kings Canyon National Park

knocked the miles down quickly. With squeals of delight, we hit the junction on time and to add celebration to the moment, the backcountry wilderness ranger happened to be standing at that junction with a ready smile and another "atta boy" to hand to the kids.

Five miles of uphill remained and surprisingly, the kids still had plenty of energy to attack the trail with vigor. When we arrived at lower Dusy Basin our "tired" kids helped set up camp and then eagerly took off to fish. At that point, Bekah hit the wall and Cade caught his second wind. Too tired to stalk fish, Bekah simply sprawled onto a large boulder on her stomach and let her fly dangle in the water as she slept. Cade was still consumed with the joy of landing prey so he stalked and crawled around the banks, successfully pulling in over twenty trout.

Too tired to celebrate or revel in our fifteen-mile victory that night, the reality of what they had accomplished didn't sink in until the next day. And when it did, I realized that our kids had been deeply affected by this extended, nearly 3 weeks on the trail.

Over the years, I have come to need these times. The few years that life circumstances did not allow us to get out for hiking trips nearly starved me. Without the chance to detoxify over the summer from the chaotic swirl of regular life, all I could do was march into fall, encumbered and heavy. Getting out on the trail seems like such a simple activity but, as in all of life, it takes intentionality. We have to carve time out of our never-ending to-do lists, gather gear, get good boots, pack a lot of food, and go. Forget the house projects. Forget the work projects. The yard will be fine. Just go!

Our intentionality started as we slogged through our first jobs after college. Cory slaved away in front of a computer all day as a civil engineer while I worked up to seventeen hours a day as a marketing and membership director at a large YMCA. These were great jobs with benefits, solid incomes, and a future. They guaranteed living well, at the top of a nice hill overlooking our holdings. But when Cory came home daily, bloodshot and lifeless, I knew something needed to change. Thirty years of that is killing people. "You come home so empty. It's like the computer hypnotizes you all day, stripping your personality from you and throwing it into the trash," I told Cory one day.

"I know. I do feel dead." He slumped on the couch and stared at the ceiling. We were so busy making money and building careers that we had no time to play and refresh. We spent a lot of times on computers and little time working with people. I missed connecting with people and feeling like I really made a difference. Cory missed the days he worked with youth at the boys camp. Living *simply* seemed so much more appealing and life-giving than this did. Our souls were suffocating.

So we gave up the good salaries, benefits, and security and went to grad school. We emerged as teachers. Teaching is frustratingly taxing and incomparably rewarding. It sucks every morsel of dedication from my marrow as every minute in front of my classes matters. Every conversation with every child matters. Every lesson plan I design and activity I implement matters. I can never go to work like I could in the good 'ole days of my YMCA office job, just having a quiet day because I showed up to work tired. Tired or not, the show starts at 8:00 a.m.

But the show ends in June. And most of us cross that finish line knowing that it's time to go home and recoup, refill, and rejuvenate so that the games can begin again in September with vigor and passion. I know that the "rest of the world" doesn't have built-in finish lines like teachers do, so their need to be intentional about carving out time to restore is even more essential because if they don't, it won't happen.

It's not happening for Ron, the kind owner of Honey Bee Septic Plumbing, who appeared on my doorstep one spring for a service call to have our septic system pumped. His kind eyes smiled when he did, but despite their twinkle, those eyes looked quite tired. When he finished his septic duties, he took a needed break from his long day and chatted about the ups and downs of his business. He leaned on his truck, exhausted. "We are heading to the lake next weekend for our first vacation in years. I haven't had a day off in seven years. Once those three days are done, I'm booked solid until January." He said this to me in April.

My heart felt for him. Granted, there is a never-ending amount of work for an owner of port-a-potties and septic pumpers (we all do, after all, keep eating), but there is a point when he will just need to say *no* to a job, pack up his truck, put on his hiking boots, and get away from it all or someday, he will have no choice.

Stress is killing our nation. According to the American Institute of Stress (2002), 43 percent of U.S. adults experience adverse health conditions due to acute or chronic stress. Moreover, an estimated 75 percent of all visits to primary care physicians are for stress-related complaints and disorders. People with high stress levels are more at risk for the common cold, heart attack, and cancer. Stress has also been linked to obesity, high systolic blood pressure, and elevated heart rates. Migraine headaches, rheumatoid arthritis, chronic fatigue, receptiveness to allergies, and other maladies are also related to chronic stress. Stress may both suppress the body's immune system and lead to hormonal imbalances that increase production of abnormal cells.

As unpleasant as that is to read, it's also alarming. We are stressed as a culture and it's making us sick. "We all need," as John Muir penned in his journal, "… places to play in and pray in, where nature may heal and give strength to body and soul alike."

We really all do need this. The years I missed backpacking weakened my body and soul. I limped through the year until the next summer when I had time to pause, pray, and be healed.

Besides backpacking, nothing has taught me more about the power of resting and repairing than yoga. I have had a love-hate relationship with yoga over the years that has finally landed on the love side. It wasn't an easy love as I am a hard core, push hard athlete. Most challenging during the hour and a half of yoga were the moments when we appeared to be doing nothing at all—or at least they used to be. My yoga instructors call it the most important minutes of the practice and often scatter long minutes of it throughout the session, telling us to lie flat on our backs, motionless. My first thoughts? *I spent fifteen dollars on this session and can go home and lie down for free. Why are we wasting class time doing this?* I was used to my runs and my power cut weight lifting class that went hard from the first moment to the last one. Now that's my money's worth.

So as I lay on my yoga mat, motionless as commanded, I wondered what good it could do. One would think that the deep stretching poses would be the most important part of a yoga practice, because it's then that it feels like you are actually doing something—and you are. But shavasana—the motionless pose—is heralded as the most important moments of the yoga practice. *Lying there doing nothing had a name?* "Shavasana is the pose of restoration," she said. It's during these quiet moments that the body has a chance to regroup and reset itself. All the work accomplished on the mat is incorporated into the body's tissues, ligaments, muscles, and organs during this rest. Without this rest, the work done during the yoga session is not as beneficial.

Psychologically, shavasana allows for a reduction in general anxiety, an increase in energy levels and productivity, an increase in concentration and memory, and an increase in focus and self-confidence. Sleep is improved and fatigue is decreased. It all sounds amazing, like something we'd expect from a health drink or the latest natural supplement. But surprisingly, these motionless pauses allow the nervous system to finally have its chance to integrate all that the body has done over the yoga session.

Years of practicing yoga has taught me this: to really rest and renew requires intention. I struggled with accepting the pauses of a good yoga practice in the beginning, but now I passionately know that everyone needs to build shavasana into their routines and into their calendars. A sabbath. A time to let the fields lay fallow.

We all really need places where we can stop and restore. As the distance from my jailhouse of fear increased, I began to taste a bit of the resting and playing and ultimately healing that comes in the beauty of being in nature—because I finally could. Holding on to fear has its own body language. Shoulders are scrunched up, brows are furrowed, the gut is tight—which all break the rules of a motionless shavasana. We can't truly rest when our shoulders are isometrically reaching for our ears and our gut is clenched in a wrestling match with our emotions. Letting go means releasing these muscles. Resting. It means releasing the brain to stop fretting... also pausing. The farther I walked from my carefully constructed courtyard of fear the more my very tense muscles relaxed and the closer I came to shavasana. Nature—and God in nature—was wowing me and filling me up, giving me perspective and replacing fear with awe. This is what rest feels like. What restoration feels like. What playing feels like!

Bekah and the Palisades, Dusy Basin, Kings Canyon National Park.

John Muir was so right. The people of the late 1800s needed it and more than ever, the wired culture of the twenty-first century needs it—shavasana—a complete disconnect from the stimuli of this world by immersing in nature. Time outside provides a brief pause for the body and soul before we are forced, once again, to deal with all the usual stresses of daily life.

Chapter 25

Doubt Defeated

Bathed in such beauty, watching the expressions ever varying on the faces of the mountains, watching the stars, which here have a glory that the lowlander never dreams of, watching the circling seasons, listening to the songs of the waters and winds and birds, would be endless pleasure.
~ John Muir, journal entry for August 14, 1869 [72]

Day 21: Dusy Basin to South Lake; 7 miles over Bishop Pass

We have not just visited, we have lived in the wilderness. The stuff of the city truly became a distant memory. The thought of turning on my phone now felt less like a promise of protection and more like a nuisance. My dreams had also radically changed: no one drove in my slow-paced dreams where the only option, of course, was walking.

As we walked these last seven miles, past some of my favorite spots, including Long Lake, I was comforted because

I knew that once we resupplied and took a few layover days, we would head back in to finish the last sixty miles.

As the second leg of our trek, a 100-mile thru-hike wound down, the family began to recount each campsite, their favorite thing about that site, their favorite day of hiking and why, and any other unforgettable moments. It was the shake down.

Without even hearing the kids' answers, I already knew which day of this second of three legs was their favorite. I could tell by the slight increase in the puff of their chests and the straightness of their backs as they stood a little taller on that last day. I could hear it in the faster pace and higher pitch as their words tumbled out. By far, the day they would remember was the day they pulled off the fifteen-mile hike, with 8,000 feet of elevation change, a difficult day even for adults.

It really wasn't until the day after their success that I could now see both Cade and Bekah's slightly taller stature. Their sense of accomplishment and success was so powerful it was simply bursting out of them. As we walked the final five miles that last day to our exit at South Lake, both kids began dreaming and planning. Excitement over huge life dreams bubbled out of them. Words came fast.

"I want to be a veterinarian for sure. What are the college classes like? Are they big classes? Maybe I could partner with another vet and we could job share so we both have more time off so I can still backpack?" spewed out of Bekah in one long paragraph that lasted for at least a mile.

Cade spent miles of trail asking about engineering, robotics, and design. "Could I design motorcycles for

Kawasaki? What about building a solar/electric car? Oh, you know what I would love to do? Work for MSR or Marmot and design backpacking equipment!" With determination, Cade announced that mechanical engineering was most definitely what he wanted to do.

Some of these were revisited ideas, expanded on and built upon, some were brand new dreams spoken for the first time, with conviction and belief in their real possibility.

As I compared trail talk on the fifteen-mile day with trail talk the day after, the notable difference was a new confidence. Endorphins mixed with the new reality that, "I just hiked fifteen miles, I did it. I wasn't sure if I had what it took, but I did—and now I'm almost done with one hundred miles (one hundred and forty miles with both trips)! I feel great and I am on my 95th mile! I can do this!" produced kids hiking down the trail who now believed they could do anything they set their minds to.

The doubt demon had been knocked down to make way for big dreams. And when it rears its ugly head again, I know that these trail lessons will kick in: perseverance, determination, sweat, and hard work got me up that mountain, so here I go, doubt and all, I am not giving up.

Another of the God rays shining down on our 200-mile summer.

Chapter 26

Our Backpacking Secret Weapon

... every crystal, every flower a window opening into heaven, a mirror reflecting the Creator... No longing for anything now or hereafter as we go home into the mountain's heart... everything is perfectly clean and pure and full of divine lessons.

~ John Muir, journal entry for July 27, 1868 [73]

❧⟩⟩⟨⟨❧

Day 22: South Lake to Dusy Basin, over Bishop Pass at 11,972 ft. 7 miles, 2100 ft. elevation change

We first met Troop #975 at Franklin Lake, in Sequoia Kings National Park, the following summer of 2013. A large group of about thirteen kids and adults, all clad in purple, showed up to our quiet lake late in the evening.

As I lazily read on our beachfront campsite, we heard one of the young boy scouts screaming from the ledge he was perched on, "Joey!"

No response prompted another, "Joey!"

Silence.

"Joey!" One final futile attempt to summon his friend came up empty.

"Maybe his name's not Joey!" I called up to the voice.

I heard a chuckle, followed by, "Jaime!" which finally instigated a response, making me laugh. After our summer of 2012 on the trail with few kid sightings, it was quite exciting to see this large purple troop loudly take over the lake. They left promptly at 7 a.m. the next day, which, sadly, did not allow us to meet their leaders. Coincidentally, a week later, the purple boy scout gang and our family reunited at Hamilton Lake—some forty miles down the trail. We quickly became friends with the leaders, Fred and Bobbi.

"This is our first backpacking trip. It's amazing out here!" Fred said with a huge smile and twinkling eyes.

"It is, isn't it? You know, a lot of troops are struggling to get boys to sign up for outings like this! I'm impressed and so proud of your group," I responded.

"I'm a bit old school and kids know that. I want them to explore, get dirty, and get outside. I think at first it makes kids skeptical, but once they taste what we do, they're hooked. Word is spreading and our troop is growing. We do an outing, many of which are overnighters, once a month. And the boys know that I don't allow them to bring a single electronic gadget. No DS. No iPods. No iPhones. Nothing. Not even for the drive. I want these boys to talk to each other… and geez, if we go through all the hassle of planning these events, I don't want them staring at a screen racing their thumbs across little machines, lost in their private world." He looked down and tapped his thumbs on an imaginary DS.

"Wow! I seldom hear that from leaders. Way to go! I so agree with that! My son doesn't even have a gaming system," I said.

"Neither does mine. And you know what's nuts? He's the only kid in his class without a gaming system. But I'd like to think that's one of the reasons he's heading into high school in the fall and he's only thirteen."

"Oh, I am sure it is. I hate to cut this short but I've got to head over to camp and get dinner going. Hopefully we'll see you guys later tonight," I said.

"Oh, yeah, I'll bring my son and daughter over after dinner to meet your kids." With that, we parted ways with a cheerful wave.

Less than ten minutes back at our camp, Fred showed up with his daughter, son, (the missing Joey from a week earlier), and a couple other eager boy scouts. Having fellow young hikers so close was obviously too tempting for the troop to wait until after dinner. An energetic conversation ensued between the scouts,the kids, and me as we shared trail stories.

Eventually I turned to Fred and asked him, "Hey, just wondering, how is your troop doing out here?"

"Oh, they're loving it. But they're pooped."

I wasn't surprised to hear that. We had hiked along side the group for a few miles and noticed that the eleven- and twelve-year-old boys had towering packs that had them bent over like Quasimodo.

"How heavy are their packs?" I asked.

"Probably thirty-five to fifty-five pounds. I know that my pack is so heavy and uncomfortable. I love the camping but I am not liking the hiking part. My knees are killing me!"

"Pack weight makes all the difference," I said.

"Do you have any advice we could pass on to the boys?" Fred asked.

"Well, I have some ideas, but the guy you want to talk to is Cory. He's hiked with youth out here for years and is a bit of a light-weight hiking guru."

I waved to Cory, who was busy fiddling with his photography equipment, over to our group. When he heard what we were talking about, his eyes lit up. I smiled knowing that this could possibly be his single-most favorite topic to talk about—especially in the mountains to a new enthusiast taking kids out with him. Their passion for the boys in their troop and the unbeatable experience the mountains provided made us want to move to San Diego so Cade could join their group.

We showed them our quarter-sized flashlights, used for night-time book reading in the real world. The boys laughed as they told us tales of their large Sherlock Holmes-sized lights. We showed them our cook kit of four bowls, four sporks, stove, and camp soap, that fit into our twelve-quart aluminum pot. Cory pointed to their heavy Nalgene bottles that they had carried up to our site. "Those bottles weigh a heavy 7 oz! Try using a cheap bottled-water plastic bottle instead and save nearly 6 oz!" The boys were eager to learn and between Fred and his little troop, we talked for at least twenty minutes. Before they left, they invited us to their camp for Cory to tell one of his infamous scary camp stories that he had perfected during his years at Pyles Boys Camp.

After dinner, we headed their way. As we entered into the clearing in the trees, I was so impressed. Scattered atop bear canisters and tree stumps sat this troop of eleven- to thirteen-year-old boys, hovered over their individual camp stoves, cooking their own dinners. Boy scouts are a boy-led, boy-run organization as was evident in the confident way each kid attended to his own dinner.

"Do they plan their own food for these trips?" I asked Bobbi as my eyes glanced around the camp.

"Oh, yeah. They sure do. They make their menus, grocery lists, and then have their parents take them shopping. Sometimes it can be hard as leaders when we see them forgetting things. It's hard to let them fail, so to speak."

"I can imagine! That would be hard!"

"We adults plan our own meals. One time, they totally forgot to pack marshmallows or chocolate for s'mores. We knew it ahead of time but didn't say anything. We got to camp and while the adults ate a delicious steak dinner complete with a s'mores dessert, they ate bland top ramen. But they learned!"

And I learned as I watched this group in action that evening. Our kids could participate more. They could learn how to run the stove and do dishes more. They could get water and do the steps needed to purify it. As their parents, all too often we just fell into the habit of taking care of these chores. They were good at setting up the tents and pulling out their sleeping bags, but they had never planned meals or made shopping lists. And it was usually Daddy who hovered over the evening dinner as it simmered on the MSR pocket rocket stove.

After Cory spooked the group with his frightening account of a part man/part wolf creature that roamed the

Sierra mountains, we said our final goodbyes. As we walked back to camp, my heart felt lighter. The community that happens naturally in the mountains when folks are not holed up behind locked doors and four walls creates evenings like this—where strangers can become quick friends and enrich each others' lives with new ideas and ways of thinking and doing.

A year earlier, on our first day back into the wilderness, Cory's light-weight neurosy made for a rather easy start to the final leg of our trek. When I commented about how easy the miles felt, Cory pointed out, "Well, we got your pack down to twenty-eight pounds, fully loaded with food; Cade's is twenty-one pounds, Bekah is at sixteen pounds, and mine is forty-two pounds."

For a six-day trip, fifty-four pounds of our total weight was simply food. I don't want to bore you with the details, as details like this can be tedious. But my point is this: we are not a superhuman family with superhero kids—even though people continued to look at us in awe as they saw us march up the hill, shouting slogans like, "you rock!" as we passed. We were generally fit and relatively strong but really, the truth, the little secret we packed in our backpacks, was that despite their girth, the packs themselves really didn't weigh much. Even so, I enjoyed the trail camaraderie with folks who appreciated the challenges of taking kids with us on a trail.

A sign at the entrance to the backpacking gear at REI asks, "What kind of backpacker are you?" and lists various tents that match up to one's style: weekend warrior to light-weight to hyper light-weight (these folks are directed to a simple tarp as they forgo a tent completely). More comfort than the hyper lights but less weight than the light-weights is where we hang out. It's simply more fun when you don't have to strain and groan up a trail. Getting to camp still smiling is a good thing!

It wasn't always this way. When the kids were babies, we nearly collapsed under the weight of our packs. With Bekah on a front pack and Cade riding the luxury line on my back in his own pack, all I could carry were a few supplies for the kids. We sacrificed Cory's knees, loading his monster backpack with ninety pounds of gear, and walked—slowly, very slowly—and I think, at times, crawled in.

Looking back, I am amazed at the lakes, fairly deep into the wildernesses, we were able to reach with our caravan. Indeed, our very young kids crawled on the shores of gorgeous high mountain lakes, but at a price, we realized, we couldn't pay for much longer if we wanted to hike much beyond their fourth birthdays.

So I went about my business of taking our babies to play groups, MOPS, and playgrounds, while Cory's engineering mind mingled with his years of experience as a boys camp wilderness guide/counselor to devise plans to reduce our loads. It was our only chance at making this sport we loved doable.

That fall, after the ninety-pound pack summer, Cory engineered, designed, and sewed our new ultra-light tents. Out went the Eureka, four-person mountain tent weighing in at nine pounds and in its place were two 2¾ pound, silnylon original creations by a desperate-to-hike dad. Lighter even than the most lightweight tents of the time weighing between

3½ and 4 pounds, he walked the trails that summer with happier knees—and a little pride sprinkled on top.

We eventually moved on to two silnylon tarp tents designed by Henry Shires. The tents are 2¾ pounds (36 oz!) a piece, sleep two comfortably, set up quickly, and even come with two roomy vestibules. Other companies are rolling out their lightweight tents every year, so these days, options abound for the lightweight packer. By 2017, we had reduced weight even more with cuben fiber backpacks and a tent, designed and sewn by Cory in his continuous pursuit of a pack-weight that won't ignite his sore hips and knees.

One night, in the early days of converting to light-weight gear, I found Cory in the garage, cutting up tuna cans. "What are you working on now, MacGyver?"

"Our new stove!" Weighing in at ¼ of an ounce, our new stove consisted of a couple of embedded tuna cans, a penny, and denatured alcohol. We used our tuna stove for years but as the kids got older and ate more, we found that the amount of denatured alcohol we needed to bring in order to cook the quantities that the four of us were eating outweighed other stoves using isobutane. We traded in our tuna stove for a MSR Pocket Rocket. It's efficiency allowed us to boil water fast, using much less fuel. Including our Pocket Rocket with fuel canister, our total cook kit weighed only 2½ pounds.

Each year we traded out a few items for their lightest possible alternative. Some years I scored a new sleeping bag, others a new light and warm jacket, and finally, I was ready to lose two pounds and trade in my super comfortable Osprey Ariel backpack for a Golite. To spread the cost out, we hit clearance sales, Craigslist, and the ever-anticipated "REI return sale" where any item that someone decided to return got sold at a deeply discounted price.

To even have a chance at this sale, we had to know exactly what we were hoping to score and once the doors opened, we needed to make a beeline to that item, using all our willpower not to get distracted en-route. This had two benefits: 1. limited options got snatched up fast so being first to the item assured it's capture, and 2. staying focused allowed us to avoid all the tempting, heavy, full-priced gadgets that lined the aisles—like allowing us to create a genuine latte on the trail—but added unnecessary pounds to our pack.

This all happened after standing in line outside the store, in near zero degree temperatures (we live in the northwest) for hours in order to guarantee our place in line. But it worked. We scored a $280 sleeping bag that weighs 1½ pounds for Cade for $19.95. Even the person at the counter had to double check that one, leaving the register for a few minutes to consult with management, only to return saying, "Okay. That's an amazing price. But it's what the tag says, so congrats on that!"

Unlike the Boy Scouts who proudly train their members to pack even the kitchen sink so "you are always prepared," we choose to find creative ways of covering all the bases so we can assure we are safe, warm, and dry, without packing the lawn chairs or the big screen TV. Ultimately, staying warm, dry, and well fed are the most important factors in staying safe on the trail.

Converting to ultra-light is not a trendy decision, but a decision based on survival. Families wanting to backpack must embrace the lightweight philosophy. Parents' packs will be unmanageably heavy if they don't. The kids won't have fun if their packs are too heavy. Ultimately, without going light, families hardly stand a chance at making a go of backpacking. Even so, there are a lot of details involved in pulling off a successful backpacking trip.

As we repacked for the third leg of our trek, we assessed our four piles of gear and found quite a few missing items. "Okay, we're missing Bekah's sock, your hiking shorts, my hiking underwear, and Cade's hat," Cory announced as he took stock of our gear piled high on the picnic table at our campground, re-packing for our final trip. We eventually located each and every item but not before chuckling over the reality that these treks require a close eye for details.

I, for one, am not too fond of detail management. It slows me down and keeps me from what I do love—connecting with people. But socks, hats, rain gear, gaiters, shoes, shorts—and on and on—is the gear world that thankfully, Cory, loves to swirl in.

As tempting as the marketing is for everything from clothing to latte machines, the real secret is that less is more. With less in our packs, we hike easier, faster, and farther so we don't even miss that martini bar we almost bought or the cappuccino kit we thought we needed. And while we are hiking we are much safer, as lighter packs mean less chances for sprained ankles and falling with a top heavy, hard-to-control pack following us around.

This is a continual work in process. Our packs that summer were not light enough so during our last layover, clothes were switched out for lighter clothes, gear was redistributed more evenly between the four packs, and some gear was left behind completely. In the end, our total pack weights dropped even lower, just in time for some insanely long uphill days that lay ahead.

Leaving the kitchen sink and the espresso machine behind meant that after ten years of refining this art of lightweight backpacking, we were still able to hit the trail (yes!) and our youngest promised that when we left the Sierras with 200 miles behind us, she would, for sure, break down in tears.

These comments had a lot of weight coming from a little girl who had just said goodbye to the grandparents she adored. Our layover with Nana and Papa hugged us close and cradled us in the delights of city life and sweet family time. Unusual daily rain and thunderstorms kept us out an extra day waiting for the weather to hopefully improve, but also allowed us more time with Nana and Papa. As always, the goodbyes were sad as we started up the trail. It was hard to leave family but they kept it fun, snapping pictures and cheering us on as we faced our last sixty-one miles. I found that once I started walking, I couldn't turn back and look at them, as it would make it more difficult to leave. We were walking back into the wilderness, with all the challenges and glory mixed together in one beautiful, colorful ball.

Their final "job" was to shuttle our truck to the Onion Valley Trailhead where it would wait for six days for our final exit. Excitement was high as we started the last of three legs, but it was accompanied with a nervous eye on the dark clouds that surrounded our trail head.

Thru-hiking versus in and out hiking over the same trail requires a support team to help shuttle vehicles or hikers. A lot more planning is involved, but we fell in love with thru-hiking, because every turn was new. Nothing was repeated as we hiked to new destinations. We were actually going somewhere!

A mile in, we could see that the clouds were dark and were gathering fast. We needed to get over Bishop Pass before any lightning started flashing. Being at one of the high spots during a thunderstorm was more adventure than this cautious mom could handle. Within the first few miles, we passed hikers heading out. The usual easy banter was replaced with solemn accounts of the trials of their rain-drenched week.

"We have never experienced weather like this in August," one hiker told us. "It rained every day, all day."

Another hiker chuckled as he recounted a few tough mornings. "We literally did not come out of our tents until after lunch, and then we only had a few hours of relief before the storms returned." Many of these hikers were cutting their trip short, officially rained out.

Should we turn back? We reasoned that we, too, could hole up in our tents and there was one trail that would lead us out early if we needed to take it. It was a challenging trail, but it was doable and would cut thirty miles off our hike. We forged on.

As we pushed toward the saddle, Bekah observed, "This is really just a day hike 'cause I spent time in a car today, was in a town today, woke up in my own bed today in our trailer... but tomorrow will be a real backpacking day!" She was onto something. The farther we are from the comforts of home, the hiker's high begins to surge through the system. Day two would be completely contained within the wilderness—from waking up on the ground to eating lunch at a stream to cooking dinner under a setting sun—when "real backpacking" would begin for our girl.

A few minutes later she added, "Hey guys, just so you know, I'm going to be real sad on the last day. There's no doubt about that!"

That summer of long miles was pulling things out of our kids that amazed me. Our daughter is one determined girl and when given high goals, such as hiking 200 miles, she stopped at nothing to make sure she accomplished what she set out to do. Up until this point in her life, she really hadn't had an opportunity to buckle down and attack a goal this large before. She rose to the occasion for her weekly spelling tests and math drills, but something that required this kind of long-term focus hadn't challenged her yet. It wasn't beating her up and frustrating her; it was captivating her. She didn't want it to end.

I quietly mused that we must be doing something right for her to feel this way. Despite just ending a fun camping layover with grandparents and having packs loaded with a weeks worth of food in bear cannisters—she expressed how much she loved what we were doing. Our son joined the parade with the same enthusiasm. He tackled each step without a complaint, creatively filling his time with rock skipping, carving, fishing, and swimming.

Boxing on the Trail

*Walk away quietly in any direction and taste the freedom of
the mountaineer. Camp out among the grass and gentians of
glacier meadows, in craggy garden nooks full of Nature's
darlings. Climb the mountains and get their good tidings.
Nature's peace will flow into you as sunshine flows into trees.
The winds will blow their own freshness into you, and the
storms their energy, while cares will drop off like autumn
leaves.*
~ John Muir, 1901 [74]

Day 23: Dusy Basin to Palisades Basin; 13 miles, 7500 ft.
elevation change

Stomping along the trail, I muttered under my breath, "I
am so mad at him!" Anger fueled, I walked faster than
normal, making it quite difficult for Bekah's nine-year-old
legs to keep up. She almost jogged behind me, in silence, with
a worried-furrowed brow. Having had a friend's parents

divorce the year earlier, she was aware, for the first time in her life, that parents can break up. Any time we fought, it terrified her. And we were fighting.

Thirty minutes earlier I had stopped to go to the bathroom. For 150 miles our practice had been to walk around the corner and wait for whoever had stopped. For some reason, that particular time there was no sign of Cory or Cade waiting for me around the corner. No writing in the dirt indicating the changed plan. No rhyme or reason for breaking from our protocol. Two minutes of hiking on the trail without the boys turned into ten minutes and then twenty minutes. I began to fume.

"Cory? Cade?" I called out into the abyss. The silent response just fueled my rising anger. "Where are you?" I called out into the trees. Nothing.

"I am so mad! Where are you?" The fact that we had spent 150 miles within 100 feet of each other sparked the fury. I was used to having Cory close and by this point in the journey simultaneously wanted him close (like a living security blanket) but was tired of it, too. A little space once in awhile is a good thing. It isn't bad to have to miss each other. And we had not been out of voice range of each other for over three weeks.

So I stomped on with Bekah nervously in tow. When nearly an hour passed without a sign of the boys, I was downright livid. Were they stopped somewhere behind us or were they waiting up ahead? Why did Cory break protocol without warning? Had something happened to Cade that made Cory take off with him, leaving him without time to tell me?

It occurred to me, as I pouted and threw my tantrum, that this was a first for me. I had spent so many years hiking with an undercurrent of fear pulsing that most other emotions could not fit. With fear diminishing every day on the other side of the courtyard wall, I had emotional space to feel pissed. Whereas before, I walked around in the mountains flat-lined and robotic. I survived. I enjoyed the experience in a middle-of-the-road way. No real highs. "It was fine, I guess," was often my response to the question, "How was your trip?"

Again, I didn't know that looking through fear-colored glasses could mute my world so drastically. I thought I saw what everyone else saw. I thought I felt what everyone else felt. How can a color-blind person, for instance, have any idea what the full-color spectrum even looks like? My emotional spectrum—when anxiety consumed the majority of it—was rather sparse. High energy emotions like anger and euphoria were crowded out. My times in the mountains often felt as if only half of me showed up for the trip.

So as I stormed the trail, it felt good in a way. It felt real. I like to fight with Cory about as much as Bekah likes to see us fight. But what he did seemed unsafe and irresponsible and uncharacteristic. At last, as if nothing had happened, we turned a corner and found the boys innocently sitting on a boulder eating Cliff bars.

I am sure Cory was caught off guard when I yelled at him. "What were you thinking? We had no idea what happened to you! I spent the last hour fretting at every corner, wondering if I took a wrong turn, wondering if something happened to one of you... why did you just take off like that without any explanation?"

"I don't know. I figured you and Bekah might enjoy some girl time and Cade and I could enjoy some guy time. I certainly didn't mean to upset you. I just get tired of all the stops we keep having. Bekah stops to fix her shoe. Then Cade has to pee. Then you have to stop to get a rock out of your shoe. I have brought up the rear of our foursome all summer and frankly, I'm frustrated at how slow we go sometimes. I just wanted to click along so when you had to stop, for the second time in thirty minutes, I just took off. I knew you'd be fine."

"We're doing our best. And I think we are doing pretty well. Geez, Cory. How about at least communicating what you're doing next time instead of ditching us without any idea of what's going on?" I said, with both fists firmly planted on my hips.

"Yeah, you're right. I'm sorry. I'm just getting tired of not putting the miles down. I'll make sure to tell you what I am doing in the future." He came toward me to pull me into a hug. I was not quite ready to let go of my tirade and stood my ground, rejecting his attempted peace treaty.

"Is that it, then? The three of us are keeping you from doing what you really want to do? You aren't satisfied with the fact that we're hiking over 200 miles for our summer break?"

"No, that's not what I mean! You guys are doing great and I love being out here with you, of course, but sometimes I just get tired of waiting all the time... "

"Let's just keep hiking. I don't really want to keep talking about it," I said, with a clipped tone. Bekah could see this wasn't resolving and took her cue to start crying. "Don't fight, Mama and Daddy. Come on, don't fight!" she pleaded desperately. It was sweet but didn't crack my ticked-off attitude. I marched past her and stormed up the trail. The gloomy mood of our tribe matched the dark and stormy skies and made for a morose hike through the LeConte Canyon.

A good hike is the perfect prescription for a bad attitude. Like a punching bag, the trail gave my body a physical place to stomp out my frustrations, most of which, I realized as the miles ticked by, were really not Cory's fault. We had spent miles of concentrated time together. A good fight forced us into our needed corners of the ring so we could have our own thoughts and much-needed solitude. And besides, sometimes a good fight just feels good.

Also unresolved were the summer storms that were not clearing up. Highly unusual weather patterns had set in, creating stunning sunsets and clouds with thunderstorms for the last eight days. Typically, t-storms slam quick, stick around for three days, and are followed by at least ten blue-sky days. As we hiked with pack covers and ponchos, I was grateful that Cory had remembered our lightweight, yet effective rain protection: pack covers coupled with a lightweight/breathable/water and wind resistant jacket and pants called Frogg Toggs. The kids simply wore ponchos that fit over their packs and covered their bodies and heads as well. Yes, details are important. It's not "good enough" if just three of us have ponchos! My first kind thought of Cory that afternoon, like a sunbreak in a stormy sky, started my heart's slow and reluctant return back to peace.

On we hiked, under a surprisingly Seattle-gray sky, from 8:15 a.m. to 6:30 p.m.—a long day even if it was spent sitting at the office! Despite the dark sky that threatened to open up its flood gate at any moment, thirty minutes was the longest we hiked in a light drizzle. We darted between storm clouds and sun breaks in perfect timing that kept us dry.

The stats of that day explained why it was the most difficult day of the summer: thirteen miles with 2700 feet of climbing over the last six miles. The last 1500 feet of the climb were so notorious that they've been nicknamed, "The Golden Staircase." Bekah counted 500 Sierra granite rock steps. With each switchback, we gained more elevation, providing for breathtaking views as we headed for the sky. The sunset's golden light pinched through the dark, heavy clouds, illuminating the rocky walls lining the heavily forested valley, creating an incredible canvas over the sweeping green valley below.

As we climbed out of the dark valley, warmer feelings continued to displace the angry cold ones. I began to feel a bit foolish for how frustrated I had been. Each step up, more anger melted away and our usual light-hearted trail talk soon filled the quiet space between us.

Around 5:30, as any working person can attest, we were all ready to be done for the day. But we had an extra late night meeting with hundreds of Sierra steps to reach the glorious Palisades Lake Basin that patiently waited for us at the end.

Once at the basin, the trail snaked through the meadow leading to the lower lake. Bekah's legs slowed down and she fell way behind, and eventually, a few tears fell. The tension of seeing us fight with this record-breaking mileage day was more than she could handle. This hike needed to end!

Everywhere we turned, we saw people camping. We had hit the section of the JMT that started to bunch hikers together, as evening destinations were more defined and obvious. The lay of the land created a typical pattern where JMTers climbed to the basin close to the next pass so that they could climb the pass the next morning.

Higher up on the hillside we found an amazing perch—one of the best of the summer—on a granite slab that overlooked the whole basin, lakes, and Palisade Ridge beyond, as well as six other groups. We all clicked into gear, deeply tired and anxious to be resting in our tents. Cade and Daddy got water while Bekah and I set up the tents. When motivated, we were quite efficient. As we finished dinner and the darkness swallowed up the last light of day, I looked over to Cory.

"Hey, sorry for getting so mad at you."

"I'm sorry, too." He put his bowl down and stood up to come over to my side.

"You just make us feel like we aren't doing good enough, like we keep you back. It makes me feel like you're always compromising. Are you going to regret having us out here with you?"

"I couldn't be a happier guy. I love being out here more than being anywhere on the planet. To get to do this with my wife and kids makes it that much better. I'd miss you guys like crazy if you weren't here. Yeah, I could go harder and faster and this morning I kinda lost sight of the bigger picture and got a bit selfish. I can't believe we are in Palisades Basin. This is a hard climb even for adults, and yet we are here together, as a young family." He directed his attention to the kids as he continued, "Kids, you are doing amazing. Today was a hard day—probably the hardest of the summer—and you tackled it in style. I couldn't be more proud of you." The kids' eyes beamed.

"Yeah, today was long, Daddy. My legs kinda hurt," Cade said.

"Mine do, too. I am so tired!" Bekah added.

Cory looked back at me as he put his arms around me and pulled me into a long hug. "Come here, hun." This time, I melted into his arms and returned the affection.

At that, Bekah's dirt-smudged and tired face broke into a smile. She put her dinner bowl down and ran over to us to jump into the middle of the embrace, noticeably relieved that we had weathered another relational storm. Cade joined us for a Brady bunch-like family group hug as the sun disappeared for good over the rugged Palisade peaks.

The next day we would climb over Mather Pass and begin meeting the strangers we saw in the distance, scattered around the basin, but first we slept hard. The trail had worn us out.

And thankfully, with all details accounted for and our skirmish resolved, we slept warm and well fed. We lugged it all up there for a reason: our evening stay at Palisades was perfectly comfortable, nestled in our warm bags, atop our air mattresses, inside our tarp tent. It took years to collect it all, not that it was really that much stuff, but it was exactly what we needed to turn any spot we landed at into our home for the night.

Trail Friends

*No man was more influential than John Muir in preserving the
Sierra's integrity. If I were to choose a single Californian to
occupy the Hall of Fame, it would be this tenacious Scot who
became a Californian during the final forty-six years of his life.
It was John Muir whose knowledge wedded to zeal led men and
governments to establish the National Park Service. Yosemite
and Sequoia in California, the Petrified Forest and the Grand
Canyon in Arizona, and the glacier wilderness of Alaska are
what they are today largely because of this one man, in whom
learning and love were co-equal. More than any other, he was
the answer to that call which appears on the Courts Building in
Sacramento: Give me men to match my mountains.*
~ Lawrence Clark Powell [75]

Day 24: Palisades Lake to Marjorie Lake; 8 miles over
12,100 ft. Mather Pass

Leap frog was the theme of the day. We were one of the
last groups to leave Palisades Basin, all headed to Marjorie
Lake in a scattered line, dotting the trail like an army of ants.
Palisades Basin was truly stunning. Close-in rugged peaks

hugged the basin that housed rolling hills of granite and grasses and a couple of sparkly lakes.

Approaching Mather Pass, Kings Canyon National Park

We fell into pace with different groups, answering the same questions with each we passed about our success and struggles of hiking with our kids. Once again, a group whipped out their cameras for proof for their own kids back home that kids really could do this. And at the top, the many groups that gathered and paused to take in the view all cheered Bekah and Cade on as we arrived. I felt a little embarrassed by all the attention and truly felt that the grey-haired folks sitting on this 12,100 foot pass had accomplished more than we had, but it's not too kosher to congratulate a 60+ hiker: "Wow! It's so good to see older people like you are out here!" So I settled for a smile and light conversation.

But truly, I loved seeing the age range that sat atop Mather pass that day—healthy, active, adventure-seeking Americans. I would love to have been able to sit and talk to each person who quietly chatted, laughed, and ate another handful of gorp. With over six different groups gathered, the reality was that many of these people most likely had overcome adversity to be able to sit in that spot, at that time, and take in sweeping vistas like those that can only be seen at 12,100 feet. Later I learned a few of the stories of the people I sat with that day: bummed knees and multiple heart stents— to name a few—were part of the full story contained in these kind-hearted fellow travelers of the trail.

Earlier in our hike we met a lady in her eighties, backpacking along with her family, like she'd done for most of her life. "Don't tell me I inspire you," she warned us. "I am just doing what I do. But you, little darling," she said, as she bent over a little to look straight into Bekah's eyes, "you inspire me!" The generations exchanged a knowing smile that said more than any words could say, and we continued on.

Yes, these happy, easygoing, fellow hikers who were cheering on our kids indeed inspired me. May I be going strong well into my gray-haired years, loving life and living it fully like these amazing people were doing.

These are the moments I loved the most about being out there. In our individual, hurried world, we live indoors, isolated from anyone we don't purposefully decide to interact with. On the trail, everyone lives outdoors. When we pass on the trail highway, we literally bump shoulders. Unlike in our cars, on the trail every person we pass we make eye contact with, smile, and often exchange a few words that sometimes leads to a full conversation. I will indeed miss the natural camaraderie created out here. A natural community.

It was a chilly and wet afternoon as we walked through the valley beyond Mather Pass, but at times the sun broke through the clouds and warmth flooded our bodies. Eventually, after walking in the rain for at least an hour, we got into camp at 3:45. Because of the unpredictable weather, we set up camp earlier than planned, close to Marjorie Lake. Soon the clouds clustered over the peaks that surrounded us and the thunderstorm officially arrived, sending the kids and me into the tent by 5:30. The evening passed slowly, as 5:30 is very early to begin a night inside a tent.

But it was all a matter of perspective. Cory hung out in the meadows surrounding our lake home in awe of the light show. I heard him say, "This is the most beautiful campsite! We can see 360 degrees of peaks!" It provided one of his most spectacular photographs of the summer with filtered light irradiating the rugged peaks as crepuscular rays aimed up, out of dark clouds. I peaked out of my tent a few times, impatiently, but succumbed to the creature comforts of my warm, dry tent.

Even now, I hardly remember this night as I spent it in a windowless gray tent, yet it is the first one Cory talks about. He saw the beauty in the storm clouds, mist, and rain because he chose a different perspective.

John Muir himself embraced whatever he faced on the trail with excitement to discover another side of nature. Stories abound of moments when he seemingly put himself in harm's way to fully experience a weather event. During one extremely wicked wind storm in the Sierras, he clambered to the top of a 100' Douglas fir tree so that he could "enjoy so noble an exhilaration of motion. The slender tops fairly flapped and swished in the passionate torrent, bending and swirling backward and forward, round and round, tracing indescribable combinations of vertical and horizontal curves, while I clung with muscles firm braced, like a bobo-link on a reed."

He wrote of this day: "One of the most beautiful and exhilarating storms I ever enjoyed in the Sierra occurred in December, 1874, when I happened to be exploring one of the tributary valleys of the Yuba River... when the storm began to sound, I lost no time in pushing out into the woods to enjoy it. For on such occasions Nature has always something rare to show us, and the danger to life and limb is hardly greater than one would experience crouching deprecatingly beneath a roof... I kept my lofty perch for hours, frequently closing my eyes to enjoy the music by itself, or to feast quietly on the delicious fragrance that was streaming past... When the storm began to abate, I dismounted and sauntered down through the calming woods... As I gazed on the impressive scene, all the so-called ruin of the storm was forgotten, and never before did these noble woods appear so fresh, so joyous, so immortal." [76]

Embracing each moment for exactly what it is means letting go of expectations of what we think we want. That night in the tent, I was wishing for the usual blue sky, warm sun that the Sierras are so famous for. I was growing weary of the colder, wet, and windy Sierras that we were encountering.

A mindset fixed on one thing—where's the sun?—did not allow me to experience that particular moment in the mountains, which will never happen again. It's a highlight of Cory's memories because he had a different mindset, one that said he wanted to soak in every morsel of the Sierras, in every mood they offered, without longing for something else.

No matter how much I sulked and wished for sun, it would not change what was to come or what was happening. I do not possess the power to change forces like this that are out of my control. I only have the power to change my own perspective.

What we do today is important because we are exchanging a day of our life for it. I exchanged a night of shooting colors, ripped peaks, and a late sunset for the gray walls of my tent. Would I ever finally get tough enough to choose the more challenging path?

Chapter 29

Passing Values to the Next Generation

Hiking - I don't like either the word or the thing. People ought to saunter in the mountains - not hike! Do you know the origin of that word 'saunter?' It's a beautiful word. Away back in the Middle Ages people used to go on pilgrimages to the Holy Land, and when people in the villages through which they passed asked where they were going, they would reply, "A la sainte terre' 'To the Holy Land.' And so they became known as sainte-terre-ers or saunterers. Now these mountains are our Holy Land, and we ought to saunter through them reverently, not 'hike' through them.

~ John Muir, quoted by Albert Palmer in *A Parable of Sauntering.* [77]

Day 25: Marjorie Lake to Dollar Lake, over Pinchot Pass; 11 miles.

Each day as we crested over a pass, we did so under mostly blue skies and a warm sun, with few scattered clouds.

As we descended and walked for a mile or two, the pass completely changed moods; dark, stormy clouds billowed around the peaks and poured over the passes. We seemed to be walking just slightly faster than the storm, which followed us every day.

We awoke to another warm, sunny morning, but clouds were already forming, warning us that we needed to move on to get over Pinchot Pass before the threat of lightning. The unusual clouds and colder temperatures created an underlying current of urgency, which trumped our normally carefree schedule that allowed for lounging on warm rocks, relishing in that "endless summer day" illusion. The constant awareness of a brewing storm propelled us forward.

Pressing on with us was the crowd we had bunched up with since Palisades Basin. For three days we leapfrogged down the trail with Scott and Tom from Santa Cruz; Fernando and his three buddies from Los Angeles; and from Boise—Paul, Beth, and their seventeen-year-old daughter Laura. There were many others on our same journey, but our pace never synced; our paths crossed briefly for a trail or weather update and then we went our separate ways. We intended to learn the stories of these three groups.

But not before they wistfully looked at Bekah and Cade and said, "You are so lucky your parents take you out here. Mine sure never did and I would have loved a chance to be out here when I was as young as you are. To be out here doing this at nine-years-old is such a privilege! You are so lucky!"

Cade and Bekah were told this so many times, they canned a response that included a smile and an, "I know." I wonder if they really did know. I wonder how they could.

Scott—of the Tom and Scott duo—told of having a dad who dropped him off at Boy Scout Camp, but never did any adventuring with him. Tom concurred; his parents never did things with him outdoors. Both men, near retirement, said they are doing things differently—purposefully and intentionally carving time out to spend on the trail with their children and now their grandchildren.

A quick reflection of childhood memories conjures up times with my parents in national parks, campgrounds, trails, and lakes, making me inwardly smile while cringing at the short 1970s shorts we all wore in the pictures. Stylish or not, those pictures catalogued our exploration of Glacier National Park; the Grand Canyon Rim; the badlands of North Dakota; Banff, Canada; Crater Lake, and many glorious places in between. With my dad at the wheel of our 1976 Winnebago, we made our way down the highways and byways of America. I don't seem to remember much else about my childhood, except these deeply etched memories of our family vacations; road trips that were telephone free, email free, mail free, and clutter free. When we pulled out of our Chicago driveway and aimed the motorhome west, we were truly disconnecting for two weeks. These were always happy times.

I didn't know it then, but I realize now that those trips out west to my dad's childhood stomping grounds in Oregon were his moments to pass on his love of place to his two kids. Raising us in the urban landscape of suburban Chicago created a disconnect between my nature-loving dad and my city-conformed one.

He grew up on twenty acres in a basic one-room cabin without running water in rural eastern Oregon. When I asked him to describe the small home that housed six kids and his two parents, he spent hours sketching out the features of his land. "Over here is where the creek ran through our property," he told me, a grin slowly spreading across his face, "and by six-years-old, I often went down to the creek, even before the bus would pick me up, and shoot us a duck. I remember bringing those early morning kills to my mom before running off to catch the bus. We'd come home to dinner of roast duck, and within a few days, the down from the feathers stuffed a new pillow." Before our talk was done, I knew where the water spigot was that filled their wash tub. I knew where they hung their game to cure and where the pigs' pen was. I knew where the makeshift basketball court was located and where the fishing holes were. After a few more promptings, he sketched out the interior workings of the cabin—an afterthought, really. Though the question that started the discussion was, "Dad, tell me about your childhood home…" his home, clearly, was never contained within the four walls of the structure on his land. His home was the creek, the dirt, the air, the animals, and the wide open spaces that surrounded the building where he slept.

Misplaced for over twenty years in the claustrophobic world of city life, my dad, shaped by his years of running free outside, was compelled to share a little of the west with his less-free kids. And as the years added up, and the trips did as well, those moments driving by, walking through, and sitting in the national parks, mountains, and rugged landscape of the unpaved parts of America did their part to effectively pass the torch of a deep love of wild places to me, a young and impressionable, wide-eyed city girl.

For the few days our paths were synced, Tom and Scott joined our efforts to help pass this same torch to Cade and Bekah. At Mather Pass, Pinchot Pass, Dollar Lake, and later Glenn Pass, we were greeted with cheers from Tom and Scott, "Go Bekah! Yeah Cade! You're my heroes!" It turns out that in all the years and hundreds and hundreds of miles they had both spent on the trail, they had never seen young kids backpacking with their families (especially for more than a night or two). They couldn't help but cheer them on, fueling the ever-growing flame inside Cade and Bekah as they made their way through 200 miles of Sierra glory.

Talks with Paul and Beth (Beth was one of only two moms I saw on the trail all summer), were varied and spread out over a few days as well. With a smiling seventeen-year-old daughter, they were just days from Mt. Whitney—the highest peak in the lower forty-eight states and the official end to their JMT thru-hike.

Years of adventures together—canoeing trips, climbing trips to Smith Rock State Park in Oregon, backpacking trips across the western states, day hiking all over Yosemite National Park—all built an inseparable bond with their daughter.

She admitted that when she hit thirteen, she was tempted to want to stay behind to get a job, hang out at the mall with friends, stay plugged in. Glancing down at her feet, she paused, remembering the pull she felt back then, but then lifted her eyes with a contagious smile. "But I never did stay home and I'm so glad. I love this!"

And I loved witnessing their family in action. A seventeen-year-old girl on the brink of her senior year in high school, in the twilight years of childhood, soon to leave the nest for college, work, and probably a family of her own, was still choosing to spend a large percentage of her summer time with her parents. She chose to forgo a minimum wage job and the extra cash that all teens love. She chose to forgo friends and shopping. Why?

Her foundational years growing up were spent side by side with her parents, exploring the wonders of nature together. Consequently, a 211-mile JMT hike won out over friends, and summer jobs, and even the chance to text! How many teens would give up texting to spend time with their parents? Laura did.

My bet is that when temptations come Laura's way, the wisdom from and trust she's built with her parents will win out again. A platform has been set—one of intentional togetherness assuring Laura that her parents aren't too busy for her; they've practiced the art of talking and listening while they spent long days and weeks together, outside, undistracted, tackling the next adventure.

There is a lot of loving, excellent parenting going on that does not require a trail. I marvel at the amazing parent/child bonds I see in my friends' families as well as my students' families. But sadly, I meet so many students whose parents are too busy sending the message through their daily, "not nows," that they are not important enough to garner their attention. At least not now. But now comes too infrequently and walls get built up between parents and their children until one day, they suddenly realize they missed half their child's life.

I have concluded that children need a bountiful supply of focused attention; in the few short years they spend in our homes, their sense of self and connection to family is built. As Tom recounted the little time he really spent with his dad, recreating, I could hear his sadness and disappointment at having been denied that time to bond with his dad. Tom only discovered the quiet, the beauty, and the exhilaration of backpacking apart from his dad on a Seattle church-sponsored high school backpacking trip.

Tom explained, "I loved the freedoms I was given, always under the covering of the two leaders. It built in me a new sense of confidence that I had never felt. Before the week-long trip was over, many of the kids (none had ever backpacked before) fell in love with it."

The unique way the group was able to bond because of the intense day-to-day teamwork required of outdoor living convinced him to change his legacy and take his own family out on the trail. The kind of lessons he learned from his youth leaders were the kind of lessons he wanted the privilege of imparting to his daughter.

Tom, Scott, Paul, and Beth all recognized that as good as intentions are at home to fully listen and focus on our kids, it proves to be nearly impossible to shut out emails, phone calls, deadlines, and meetings, and have time left over after good things like soccer and piano. Our own admitted weakness to the trappings of this world are part of what creates the strong pull to a wilderness devoid of all of these daily distractions.

Fernando was easy to find as his pack glistened in the sun with a large solar panel affixed snuggly on the top. At a river crossing I asked him, "Are you solar powered?"

"Kind of. I couldn't be out here without my iPod or iPhone. The panels keep them charged," he explained. "I watched *Star Trek* last night."

Cade's eyes grew large at the mention of such an option. This guy hiked in style. Just not our style.

Friendly banter passed between our two groups off and on for days. Fernando's amiable manner made us smile each time we met. An electrical engineer with the Department of Defense, Fernando had not only served overseas, he had also served time with search and rescue crews. He had witnessed every kind of emergency possible and each time, he added more equipment to his pack, ensuring he was prepared for anything.

"Yeah, I promised these grumpy old mens' wives I'd get them home safely," he joked as he pointed to the three older guys standing with him.

Rod, one of those very grumpy old men, ribbed back, "We have no idea why he lugs all this stuff out here. He's nuts."

Fernando's gang of grumpy old men were all retired from the military, one an ex-Navy Seal. All carried large, military style packs, various bodily ailments, and memories of overseas combat. They might have joked about Fernando's excessive pack, but in reality, they all succumbed to their military training to come prepared, at all costs. And despite their continual jabs at each other, it was clear they had each other's backs. It's why Fernando lugged items like a heavy two-pound climbing rope, bear spray, and two large sheathed knives—so he'd be able to get his buddies to the trailhead alive as promised.

Turns out, they almost needed that rope. As Fernando met up with us at a watering stream, he explained a frightening moment that had just happened. "Mike, the Navy Seal, has bad knees, one worse than the other. In order to momentarily reduce pressure on one of his knees, he decided to use his good leg to push off a boulder lining the trail. The boulder gave way and he fell over the edge, about a six-foot drop. Thankfully, he landed on a ledge or his fall might have been fatal as he would have dropped 30 feet or so into the river below."

Whoa. That was a sobering moment. Fernando hiked past us and then stopped and turned back. Lightening the mood, he added, gently ribbing us light-weight packers "See, I almost needed that rope!"

I smiled back. "I guess the real trick is to just hike near you, in case of an emergency, that is. After all, you're carrying whatever we'd potentially need."

Then he casually tried to unload some weight on us. "You want some bear spray? I brought two cans. You can have one… seriously."

"Hey, thanks, but we're fine."

"Are you sure? Really, you can have it!"

We smiled and declined, waving as we passed.

At 6:30 p.m., we found ourselves still hiking. Seven hours earlier we crested Pinchot Pass and hit a long section of downhill trail that bordered Woods Creek. The air was warm, but with a cool breeze, and dark clouds, once again, were forming where we had just come from, chasing us down the JMT with a daily urgency. The downhill ended at a 100-foot long suspension bridge, hanging twenty-five feet over Woods Creek. The intimidating bridge swayed three feet in each direction, underscoring the sign that warned hikers to travel the bridge one at a time.

As groups gathered on each end waiting their turn to cross the bridge, time slowed down. Some miles on the trail are mindless; others, like these, are highly calculated, as slipping meant certain death. When pushed to our limits, these are the moments that are most remembered.

Safely across, we had our final words with Fernando and his group: Rod, Danny, and Mike. The notion that we could hike near them didn't pan out as their gear-heavy pace was more of a leisurely stroll compared to our spirited one. After the bridge, we never saw them again.

If they are still out there, I know they are comfortable, safe, and perfectly prepared. They are probably grilling hamburgers and drinking cold beers. With their solar panels and iPhones, they are able to text home every day, assuring worried wives that all's well. And they never have to miss an episode of *The Office*! Bonus!

We enjoyed our banter with these highly prepared military men. The truth is, they've seen more than anyone should ever have to, and I really do understand their paranoia-driven need to pack heavy. Because of my history with seizures sixteen years ago, we have a one-way satellite PLB (personal locator beacon), usable just one time, but if we push the button, a distress signal is sent on the standard Search and Rescue frequency, and our gps coordinates are included to help with location. $250 for this gadget is well worth our peace of mind. In later years, we'd upgrade to the In Reach Delorme satellite system that allows for outgoing and incoming emails as well as an emergency call button to search and rescue. We all have different levels of comfort and there is no need to sacrifice to the level that one would feel scared and unprepared. It's a balance between that and keeping packs as light as possible.

At the suspension bridge we parted ways with Fernando and his band of merry men and began our climb up to Rae Lakes Basin, one of the most popular basins in the Sierras. At 6:25 pm, we were exhausted and still two miles shy of our destination. We had been hiking uphill for hours and were so ready to rest for the night. As we turned the corner, Dollar Lake, a small, pristine lake nestled in the trees, came into view.

No sooner had we spotted the lake than we heard a call from within the forest.

"Hey Bekah! Hey Cade! You made it!" It was our favorite cheerleaders again, Tom and Scott.

"Hi, guys! When did you get here?" we asked.

"Oh, about thirty minutes ago. Are you hiking on?"

"Oh no… just looking for a campsite. Any will do."

"Why don't you stay here?" they suggested. And so we did. The Tom and Scott campground was just what we needed. This trip, with a pass each day and over ten to fifteen daily grueling Sierra miles was proving to be our most challenging, yet beautiful, stretch of our summer trip.

Those last sixty-one miles of our summer trek had 30,000 feet of elevation change. Walking downhill, controlling a pack was a quad burn and walking uphill was a total body burn, including a cardio challenge. Scott and Tom were feeling it, too, they admitted. We scanned our eyes around the lake and realized that this was a magnet for many of us feeling the same muscle burn; the lake was a packed house, full of hikers stopping just shy of Rae Lakes.

We had two more passes after Dollar Lake, leaving just one more night before our 200-mile summer concluded. The multiple groups we intersected with as we journeyed that dirt path underscored the truth that everyone out there had their own unique ways of accomplishing their trips. There was no one right way to pull this off. Each added his or her own personalities, strengths, and weaknesses into the mix as they attacked their goals. One guy we met was attempting to hike in the style of John Muir, with just Little Debbies (Muir's bread) and an electrolyte drink (Muir's tea).

Meeting each group and hearing their stories of how and why they hiked made our time on the trail that much more rich. I thought of how life could take unexpected twists and turns—sometimes through sheer happenstance, like running into the Fernando troupe at a stream crossing—sometimes through calculated decisions, like mine to keep hiking, despite bouts of crippling fear. Or Laura's to choose a summer with her parents over a summer with her friends. In the end, it could all be called fate, but to me, it was all intentional; decisions made along the way by strangers that lead us to cross paths so that we could learn from each other.

Chapter 30

Siblings with a Different Tune

*But to get all this into words is a hopeless task. The leanest
sketch of each feature would need a whole chapter. Nor would
any amount of space, however industriously scribbled, be of
much avail. To defrauded town toilers, parks in magazine
articles are like pictures of bread to the hungry. I can write only
hints to incite good wanderers to come to the feast.*
~ *John Muir, 1901* [78]

Day 26: Dollar Lake through Rae Lakes area over Glenn
Pass to the Bullfrog Lake area

Our last night was in my favorite meadow, just outside
Bullfrog Lake which is so popular and gorgeous that for the
last twenty-five years, rangers have prohibited all camping in
that area. To get there we traversed through the gorgeous Rae
Lakes Basin which felt like walking into a postcard, with
numerous lakes at various elevations, unforgettable moments
in its beautiful grip. Trails wound through the basin past

pockets of flowers and along the shores of sparkling waterways. Eventually, the trail began to ascend the rugged white granite, steep terrain that we had seen in the distance. We climbed over Glenn Pass, considered by some to be the most difficult pass on the JMT. And indeed it was rugged, full of boulder fields to traverse in an endless uphill pursuit of the top.

Rae Lakes Basin has multiple approaches and is part of several loops, making it the most crowded section of trail we encountered all summer. We met more JMT thru-hikers, now just days from the official Mt. Whitney end, sporting huge smiles knowing their end was in sight: they were about to accomplish their 211 mile JMT thru-hike goal. We even crossed paths with a couple spending their Sunday ultra-mile running the forty-five mile loop from Kings Canyon National Park up through Rae Lakes and back to Kings Canyon. Surrounded by highly motivated, active, smiling folks, it seemed that America was full of slim, fit athletes. We shared the euphoria of standing atop the rugged Glenn Pass overlooked Rae Lakes basin to the north with Tom and Scott and at least ten other JMT through hikers.

After our final goodbyes to Tom and Scott, we made our way to our final campsite of our second leg, near Kearsarge Lakes. As Cade had lived without walls all summer, he was no longer satisfied to just cross streams or walk besides lakes as a passive observer of his surroundings. With his homemade willow rod, he headed straight to the stream near camp after setting up his home for the night. He had become a student of fish behavior, stalking them in a crawl or crouched position

Climbing Glenn Pass.

in the tall weeds, along the banks, becoming a little expert on fish habits. Consequently, his hours in this fish classroom awarded him with nearly twenty catches since his first catch in Franklin Meadows. He figured out how long to let his fly land on the water, how to wriggle it just right to mimic a real bug, and which fly from his collection (fellow hikers and fly fishing aficionados could not resist donating flies to his cause) was the best match for the evening's hatch. By the following summer he was catching as many as 90 trout in an evening.

In this setting, Cade had time to focus on Bekah a little more. "Bekah, I so badly want you to catch a fish! The feeling is incredible!" Cade announced to his discouraged fellow fisher lady, who had not yet caught one. If it was to happen, it would have to happen that night, as it was our last. We all rooted for her.

That last night I was a keen observer of a brother who was willing to look beyond himself and help his sister catch her first fish. He clearly was the resident expert in Bekah's mind, so she dropped to her knees and crawled along the bank for hours, mimicking her brother.

I am not sure whose squeals were louder, Bekah's or Cade's, when at last, Bekah landed her first fish: a 5" brook trout. Success felt good.

Cade and Bekah bonded in ways they just couldn't seem to in the busyness of home life. Built on shared experiences of teamwork toward a common goal, they now had thousands of memories together. Everything from the giggles over gaseous emissions wafting in their shared tent to the high-fives at the top of another challenging pass to setting up a tent together had formed the foundation to what we hope will be more than just a sibling relationship, but a real friendship. I was deeply touched as I saw the bonds forming between brother and sister.

Chapter 31

The Last Day

I am just a tiny person... but there is a place for me and for everybody, to sit down on this earth and touch it and call it their own.

~ Mma Ramotswe, *The No. 1 Ladies Detective Agency* [79]

❧

Day 27: Bullfrog Lake area over Kearsarge Pass to Onion Valley Trailhead; an easy 7-mile ending

Our first warm morning in many days hugged us sweetly as we breakfasted for the last time. A quiet sense of awe mixed with sadness that our 200-mile plus summer really was almost over. A thin brown ribbon of dirt that weaves inconspicuously through the Ansel Adams and John Muir wildernesses, connecting Yosemite National Park to Kings Canyon National Park had tied our world together for four weeks.

We had one more easy pass between us and our truck. Kearsarge Pass at 11,720 feet would be our last chance to look back over the massive peaks and lakes of the Sierras.

We took our time getting on the trail, choosing to linger longer on warm granite rocks, taking in the sights, smells, and feel of a Sierra morning… one last time.

One last time to listen to a stream bubble up and gurgle by.

One last time to hear nothing but birds, wind, and trees.

One last time to watch the light glow on this famous Range of Light.

The hike to the top of the pass was fast. Seven miles to the truck was all we had left with only a couple of miles to the top of one of the easiest passes to climb. We had light packs and our strongest legs of the summer. It struck me as ironic that our strongest summer legs and our lightest packs were wasted on the easiest pass. The kids and I reached the summit in no time. At the top, we looked down the trail to see Cory, paused, looking back at the beauty we were leaving behind. When he finally reached the summit, he was quiet and introspective. His shoulders were hunched slightly forward making his tall stature seem shorter. Classic wistful signs. I could tell by looking at him that the excitement of the moment was tangling with genuine sadness.

But a cheerful crowd gathered at the top snapped him out of his reflective state. With a delightful southern drawl, Chris' animated enthusiasm was the perfect greeting for us as we left our beloved Sierras behind. "This is my first hike out here ever! I moved to California from Kentucky just for this. No other reason. Just these mountains. This is unreal! I can't stop taking pictures. Every turn I think it's amazing but then I walk up a little farther and it's even better, so I snap another picture." Chris was radiant. He literally jumped as he spoke, his animation and run-on sentences underscoring why we did this at all.

Such a fitting way to end our adventure. We were handing a baton off to someone who was on day one of his discovery of a place we had come to call our home away from home. *Here you go, Chris. Here's the baton. We just finished, now it's your turn to explore. Enjoy! Be aware: you will be changed.*

As we prepared to embark on the five miles we had remaining, we took one look back over the valley. I said goodbye and thought: The day we walk over this pass without stopping to let these mountains and lakes impress us, that's the day we've grown too hard to see God in this.

Those final five miles were easy, downhill all the way to the truck. We passed two lovely lakes that fed rushing waterfalls plunging over more ripped landscape. It made me smile. The Sierras delivered raw beauty through the last step.

As promised, upon passing the sign that marked the boundary to the John Muir Wilderness, Bekah began to cry. "I am so sad it's over. I don't want to leave the Sierras," she said through her tears as we snapped our last photo.

We all felt it. We were charmed by this place, yes, but more than that, we lived outside, working as a team, bonding, talking, laughing, and even being quiet, as we walked our summer away in slow motion, together.

Chapter 32

Perspective from 2 1/2 mph

Look at that sea, girls—all silver and shadow and vision of
things not seen. We couldn't enjoy its loveliness any more if we
had millions of dollars and ropes of diamonds.
~ Lucy Maud Montgomery, *Anne of Green Gables*

Hiking changed me. The contrast between life in Chicago and life on a mountain trail is profound. That contrast illuminated truths that resonated at the core of who I was created to be. It taught me what peace felt like. Of what joy without fear felt like. Ultimately, it took the very thing that shackled me with the ball and chain of fear to free me from its tyranny. Our hike narrated a powerful story of what can happen when, from time to time, we live without walls.

Within 200 miles, with a two-foot wide dirt trail as our guide, we learned how to treasure again. How to wonder again. How to simply "be."

Each time I walk back in, I wrestle with letting the calm of the wilderness pull me away from a manic desire for doing into a place of just being.

Growing up in the cement jungle of Chicago, I never realized the emotions I feel each time I find myself in the quiet of nature were possible. But they are. It's peace defined: clear-minded thinking, a redefined perspective underscoring connections to others above to-do lists, a sobering picture that nature in all its grandeur and beauty marches on whether or not our all-important agendas do, an inner calm as we hear our own thoughts again.

My uncle Tim lives for bow hunting season. Come August, he is loading his beat up 1982 blue F-250 truck with all the supplies he will need for life in the woods for the month of September. He spends all year planning, preparing, and dreaming of this month that he gets to live with his brothers and life-long friends in the same woods he has gone to for forty years. He told me about one particular warm, blue sky day in early September, when he found himself, like he often did in September, observing the quietness of the woods from his stealthy position in his tree blind. Far removed from his day job working in a sugar-beet factory in western Idaho, he waited for his deer to walk into range. His mind drifted to the radio announcement he had heard that morning: record high lottery, it had boasted. Get your ticket today! And with little else to do, he let his mind wander to what life would be like with millions in the bank, which led him to this question: "Where would I be, right now, if I won?"

Uncle Tim's story returned to the hunt at hand, talking of all the vivid details that keep him coming back for more every year. Something stirred the forest floor, triggering an instant hopeful alertness. Leaves crunched and twigs snapped, but alas, the culprits were revealed to be two curious squirrels chasing each other from tree to tree. When he went back to his millionaire dreams, he realized, "Geez, I'd still be right here! I love this! When I am here, I *am* a millionaire. It's where I'd be if I had all the money in the world."

That is a good feeling. To want for nothing is unbeatable. Perhaps this is the core of what peace feels like: to want for nothing!

John Muir echoed my uncle's sentiments one hundred years earlier when he penned, "Days in whose light everything seems equally divine, opening a thousand windows to show us God. Nevermore, however weary, should one faint by the way who gains the blessings of one mountain day; whatever his fate, long life, short life, stormy or calm, he is rich forever." [80]

We wanted our children to taste, smell, and experience such wealth. I wanted this to root deep in the very tissues of their bodies. In my own body. Have something we could connect to when life's pace became reckless, when our centers felt off balance.

The very din of our man-made distractions prevent us from hearing, feeling, seeing, enjoying. That din can keep us from knowing ourselves. It can keep us in a perpetual state of adrenaline. It can keep us running from our fears instead of facing them.

But oh, to discover, together as a family, what life is like without the din is priceless. And that is exactly what we discovered.

Because we decided to give it a shot, go for it, and trade in racing through life for a summer at 2½ mph.

Epilogue

⟶⌃⟵

60 miles from Onion Valley to Mt. Whitney and then out
Cottonwood pass

On a warm, blustery late July afternoon three summers
later in 2015, we were bustling around camp on the edge of
Guitar Lake—*the* Guitar Lake—the staging area to summit
the infamous, tallest mountain in the lower 48 and official
end to the JMT—Mt. Whitney. On our boots was dust from
the once-intimidating Forester Pass that dangles over the
valley floor at 13,153 feet high. We had walked every inch of
this trail and the only thing left to do was this final climb.

Gazing from our perched campsite high on the northern
rim, we could see at least a hundred people dotting the
landscape. The air was palpable with excitement, though I
looked for any signs that fear hovered over those colorful dots
walking the shores like it did with me.

That pesky trail-mate was still tagging along. It camped
right on my shoulder and on cue, did what it does best:

panicked when traversing exposed ridges, begged for us to quit, and on and on. Sometimes, when the trail miles got long and we had some time, I talked to my uninvited hiking partner.

I asked, "Would you like me to sit down, right now, in the middle of this trail and stop moving?"

To my surprise this hiking partner screamed, "Yes!"

"Well, we can't do that or I'll starve to death. How about you just come along and do what you do. But recognize that I am in charge and my legs will keep walking."

So, we did this awkward dance together all the way down the trail and as we sat together under the massive gaze of this mighty mountain, my hiking partner yelled loudly, jumped up and down, and threw trail mix in a fury.

"Hitchcock Lakes" by Cory O'Neill, Sequoia National Park

Images of Bekah or Cade slipping to their deaths right in front of me flashed through my mind and crashed into images of me... passing out or having a seizure from the highest altitude I had ever experienced overwhelming my system. At moments like that, my hiking mate was more like a massive and threatening monster. I thought I was past this. I thought I was a courageous and seasoned hiker. Why was *he* still here?

Courageous hiking - courageous living - involves dancing with fear as it pushes us into the unknown. But at the end of the day, courageous living involves letting the wonder of the unknown propel us forward. I sat at the end of this hike realizing that I needed to stop denying that this hiking partner named fear was a part of the journey and stop feeling ashamed because he was part of the group. He came along and said his piece but it would always be my decision not to let him define me. He could come on the hike—in fact, he would come on the hike—but he could not stop me from summiting Mt. Whitney. Actually, his company made the whole experience more real, more alive, and that much more exciting. This wasn't small stuff we were about to do. Having the infamous hiking partner *Fear* on the journey was proof that we were doing something grand.

When the 1909 stone sheltering hut on top of Mt. Whitney came into view less than twenty-four hours later I caught a glimpse of tears rolling down Cory's cheek as I wiped my own damp eyes. As the kids scrambled to the top of a granite slab and threw their hands up in triumph, I knew for certain why we had fought so hard to be there. With the clarity of the Sierra sun, I knew we were all called to do this. That hard-earned peak we stood on together, united by the the challenges and the victories of hundreds of trail miles as a family. Victory is powerful. Shared victory is life-changing. Experiencing that moment on top of the world for the first time with two beaming kids on a cloudless July day, all the lessons of the trail were driven deep into our beings, permanently becoming part of who we are.

And who we are together.

Summit of Mount Whitney, Sequoia National Park

Appendix

Eating on the Trail

What We Eat

Breakfast: homemade granola with various seeds and nuts; oatmeal/cream of wheat; protein drinks (we like Trader Joe's hemp protein mix and Prozone, a balanced mix of carbs, protein, and fats without the use of soy).

Lunch: dehydrated hummus and dehydrated salsa with chips (dehydrated before the trip); sausage and cheese (nitrite and nitrate free sausages are cheap at Trader Joes); raw crackers and raw fruit bars (recipes at end of chapter); peanut butter and jelly, crackers and bread.

Dinner: dehydrated dinners (made ahead) stocked with meats and organic veggies; freeze-dried meals.

Snacks: dried fruits and nuts; Gorp (nuts, seeds); raisins, dried fruit, and a touch of dark chocolate chips; dark chocolate bars; power bars (we try to avoid soy-based ones); Greens First drink; Oreos!

272 / *Living Without Walls*

Fuel to move is a huge component of a successful trip. We are careful not to choose food based just on calories but instead chose nourishing food. The rule of thumb is that each person on the trip will eat about 1½ to two pounds of food per day. If we are going to lug it up the mountain, we want to make darn sure that those pounds of food packed some good nutrition. Kids fueled by balanced nutrition have the components they need to happily scale a pass, hop over boulders, and set up their tents. We whine because we are uncomfortable. Whiney, complainy trail kids might just be a product of poor nutrition. As teachers we see it in our classrooms all the time. We need to set our kids up for success, not failure.

Talking about food hits at a personal level. There are probably as many perspectives on what to eat as there are people on a trail. John Muir himself reportedly lived on tea and bread, but often wrote of feeling weak from hunger, choosing to feast on the beauty around him. I am not as brave as Muir to attempt to hike hungry and weak.

A competitive athlete since I was eleven has always required a close examination of the food passing by my lips. Before I took a single class in nutrition or exercise science, my coaches in high school and college insisted that we abstain from soda and greatly limit our sugar intake during our running season. I didn't know why, but I listened to them anyway. Not until I pursued an undergraduate degree in Exercise and Sports Science and a Masters degree in Health Education did I start to understand the connection with nutrition and performance.

Staying away from colorful, packaged food is the key. Food that looks exactly as it did when it grew is ready to knock our socks off with all of its goodness. Bright orange carrots, dark green leafy kale, and bright red juicy apples are just a few tempting examples of the variety available on our little planet. A planet packed with food as medicine. A body filled with a continuous supply of nutrients, minerals, and enzymes is energized and able to take on more than just surviving each day.

I know first hand that the years we were sick, our focus was in surviving each day; dreaming about future adventures was the last thing on our minds.

Cory and I have both overcome health issues that the medical community promised we'd deal with for the rest of our lives, even with the drugs they wanted to prescribe. We were both told that what we ate would not make a bit of difference in overcoming our health problems. But because of changes we made to our diets, we watched and felt our bodies surge a response and emerge victoriously healthy.

I love a good treat as much as the next person. However, I find that keeping intake to a minimum reduces the incessant craving for more. A simple chocolate nugget can satisfy. In her book *Lick the Sugar Habit*, Nancy Appleton, PhD, makes a compelling case against too much sugar in our lives. She lists seventy-six reasons to kick the habit, one of which is particularly important for athletes on a trail: sugar upsets the mineral relationships in the body, causes chromium and copper deficiencies, and interferes with absorption of calcium and magnesium.

Other significant findings Nancy listed that are directly related to children are:

~ Sugar can cause can cause a rapid rise of adrenaline, hyperactivity, anxiety, difficulty concentrating, and crankiness in children.

~ Sugar can cause drowsiness and decreased activity in children.

~ Sugar can interfere with the absorption of protein.

~ Sugar can make our tendons more brittle.

~ Sugar is an addictive substance.

~ High sugar intake can cause epileptic seizures (a good one for me to note!)

~ Children in juvenile rehabilitation camps put on a low sugar diet had a 44 percent drop in antisocial behavior.

After a constant intake of veggies and fruit to energize us during the nine months we are planning for our backpacking trips, it serves to reason that it would take as much, if not more, of the same power-packed food to keep us invigorated for a highly athletic summer. While ingenious, carrying a long extension cord to power a fridge to keep raw foods fresh did not jive with our lightweight philosophy. We opted for making veggie packed dinners in our kitchen at home and dehydrating those meals on our Excalibur nine-tray super dehydrator. Some nights we got into camp late and had to rely on the quicker freeze dried meals, but these never settled as well as the real food coming from our own kitchen did.

The dehydrator whirred 24/7 in the months leading up to our departure as swiss chard, fruit bars, hummus, salsa, and dinners all gave up their water so that we could pack them along and take in their goodness months later. Some may find this laborious but I found it a fun way to spend the dark winter months: preparing for our summer fun. It's not as difficult as it may at first seem. I simply tripled or quadrupled my recipes—so we'd eat a serving in February and have it again in July.

"Drink your salad!" became the daily affirmation to our meals as we each drank a serving of a green drink packed with veggies and nutrients that were difficult to come by on a trail. We often drank a protein drink as well, choosing between either a rice-based or a hemp-based formula.

Taking the time to focus on not just the raw calories needed for a hike (or a day at the office) but instead on the actual nutritional needs made for happy, healthy, vibrant people.

So much good information is available. If you find yourself reading this and thinking you need to make some changes, I encourage you to check out some books and start learning. In the meantime, by avoiding processed foods and shopping in the produce section of your grocery store, you will be off to a great start.

Kris Carr summarizes the goal. "By increasing the amount of raw and living foods and organic green juices and green smoothies in your diet while decreasing or (ideally) eliminating processed sugars, refined starches, animal products high in saturated fat, stimulants and too much cooked food, you shift from an acidic interior environment to one that's alkaline-and-oxygen-drenched. Yummy. This allows your body to recover from the constant barrage of stress and inflammation created from the Standard American Diet (aptly abbreviated as SAD) and lifestyle. Once your body repairs, it will renew. Eating this way is a miracle on your plate. The domino effect that will occur will influence every nook and cranny of your life."

We have not completely recreated our menus on the trail to mirror those of our off-trail lives. Unable to eat raw organic veggies out here on a daily basis, we compromise with a green powder drink. Burning calories at the rate that we do on the trail requires an addition of high-fat sausage, but we choose nitrite/nitrate free ones.

The myth that what we eat doesn't affect us too much is long gone. Everything we choose to eat does something in our bodies. Either our body is nourished by it or it has to deal with it. And since we have to find room in our packs for every morsel of food, everything we bring is scrutinized. Why pack a Snickers bar if we can pack a fruit and nut bar in its place?

Our meals are made ahead of time and dehydrated to be rehydrated on the trail. This allows for trail meals to be nutritious, delicious, and enjoyable. Really, most things can be dehydrated. Eat a serving in February and eat it again in July!

Preparation:

> ~ For a dehydrator, I highly recommend Excalibur with Teflon liner sheets for each tray.
> ~ A regular oven works, too, with the food on cookie sheets and temperature set between 140 F and 165 F,

keeping door slightly ajar. This requires constant vigilance. You can't leave the house like you can when using a dehydrator. The contents need to be stirred more frequently when using the oven.

~ Spread the meals on the tray no thicker than ¼ of an inch.

~ Shred all meats such as pork and chicken for better dehydrating. These meats take longer to rehydrate. Allow an hour at camp for these meats to be ready to eat.

~ Ground turkey, we have found, does not dehydrate and rehydrate well. Ground beef works much better.

~ Cook and dehydrate ground beef separate from other ingredients. Rinse ground beef after it's cooked to reduce the amount of fat on the beef. This allows the beef to store longer without a risk of going rancid. It will have the texture of gravel when dehydrated correctly.

~ Store dehydrated meals in Ziplock bags, labeled with meal names, number of cups of pre-dehydrated food in the bags, and date bags were filled. Our family of four needs to dehydrate meals in eleven-cup quantities.

~ Squeeze out all air before sealing the Ziplock bags. Consider using oxygen absorbers for longer term storage or if food is being shipping ahead for thru-hiking. See: www.rainydayfoods.com and www.sorbentsystems.com

~ Store in freezer for up to eight months.

~ Double check all meals before taking them; discard meals with any sign of rancidness or mold, which means they weren't fully dehydrated.

Campsite Cooking

At camp, empty ziploc bag(s) of dried food into pot and fill with water to the amount written on the bag. For example, if the ziploc bag is filled with ten cups of cooked meal, fill the pot to a total volume of ten cups.

~ Heat ingredients to boil, then turn off heat. Let soak for thirty minutes to one hour, keeping an eye out for bears and other critters!

~ Reheat if necessary and serve!

~ After cleaning pot, remember to bury all dishwater at least 200 feet from streams and lakeshores in a hole at least ten inches deep.

The following recipes are some of our family favorites. Hopefully, they will inspire you to create your own; the possibilities are endless!

Breakfast

Morning Sunshine Granola (makes about 5 cups)

1½ c regular rolled oats
½ c slivered almonds
½ c coconut
½ c toasted wheat germ
½ c sesame seeds
½ c sunflower seeds
½ c honey, agave nectar, or coconut nectar
⅓ c orange juice

1. In an extra-large mixing bowl combine oats, almonds, coconut, wheat germ, sesame seed, and sunflower seeds.
2. Stir together syrup or honey and orange juice. Pour over oat mixture, stirring till coated. Spread mixture evenly in a greased 15x10x1 inch baking pan. Bake in a 300 degree oven for 45 to 50 minutes or until brown. Stir every 15 minutes until the last 15 minutes when it's best to stir more frequently. Add ½ c raisins or dried fruit if you like.

Coconut Granola

We love this granola! You will not be disappointed. It's worth the extra work to secure the coconut sugar and oil. A taste of the tropics on the trail!

2 c old-fashioned rolled oats

¾ c shredded sweetened coconut

½ c chopped raw almonds

⅓ c raw pumpkin seeds

2 tbsp coconut sugar

1 tsp cinnamon

¼ tsp salt

4 tbsp coconut oil, melted

½ c pure maple syrup

1 tsp vanilla extract

¼ tsp almond extract

1. Preheat oven to 300 degrees. Line a large baking sheet with parchment paper and set aside.
2. In large bowl, combine oats, coconut, almonds, pumpkin seeds, coconut sugar, cinnamon, and salt.
3. In small bowl, whisk together coconut oil, maple syrup, vanilla extract and almond extract.
4. Pour liquid mixture over dry ingredients. Stir until dry ingredients are well coated.
5. Pour onto lined cookie sheet and spread out into an even layer.
6. Bake for 30 minutes, stirring every 10 minutes.
7. Let cool and then store in Ziplock bags.

Lunch or Snacks

Raw Crackers

I remember sitting and sharing the experience of a gorgeous pass in the Sierras with two doctors from Southern California. They were curious about our unique looking crackers, so we let them taste them and then couldn't stop raving about how delicious they were. Our kids eat these up faster than they eat a salad, and in effect, it is a crispy salad.

Having a Vitamix or Blendtec blender is a huge help with these crackers as it's important to liquefy all ingredients.

Raw BBQ Doritos

1 c golden flaxseed
1 c carrots
2 garlic
1 c raisins (pre-soaked for 15 minutes)
1 celery
4 or 5 tomatoes
a handful of sun dried tomatoes
salt to taste
chili powder to taste

1. In a bowl, soak flax seed in water and set aside.
2. Fill your Vitamix blender (or other high speed blender) halfway with water. To the blender add all ingredients (except flax seed) and blend until creamy.
3. Pour the creamy mixture into a bowl. Add 5 huge spoonfuls of the now gelatinous golden flaxseed to the creamy mixture.

4. With a spoon, spoon dollops of the mixture onto the Teflon sheets of your dehydrator to make round crackers.

5. Dehydrate for 5 to 6 hours or until crispy. Flip each cracker and dehydrate for a couple more hours.

Onion Ring Crackers

1. Slice sweet onions or red onions into nice onion rings.

2. Pour the BBQ batter on onions.

3. Put the onions with the batter on them on the Teflon sheets on the dehydrator.

4. Dehydrate for 4 to 5 hours, flip if necessary, and dehydrate for a couple more hours.

Corn Chip Raw Crackers

1 c corn

1 celery

2 to 4 tbsp of golden flax seed

1 tomato

2 garlic

4 green onions

½ tsp salt

1 to 2 c of raw walnuts pre-soaked in water

1. Fill the Vitamix or other blender halfway with water. Add all ingredients except walnuts, and blend until liquefied.

2. Add the walnuts and keep blending.

3. Spoon out nice round dollops of your mixture onto Teflon sheets on the dehydrator.

4. Dehydrate for 4 to 5 hours and then flip each cracker and dehydrate for a couple more hours.

Julie's Crispy Raw Crackers

8 tbsp golden flaxseed, soaked in water for 20 minutes

1 c carrots

3 plum tomatoes

2 garlic cloves

1 c raisins, soaked in water for 20 minutes, drained

½ c to 1 c of raw walnuts soaked in water for 24 hours, drained

1 c organic sundried tomatoes soaked in olive oil

2½ tsp of chili powder (more or less to your taste)

Salt to taste

1. Fill the Vitamix or high-powered blender half full of water. Add all ingredients except flax seed and blend.

2. Pour the batter into a large bowl. To the batter add the golden flaxseed, which will be gelatinous.

3. Spoon the batter onto the Teflon sheets in nice round dollops.

4. Dehydrate for 6 to 8 hours. Flip each cracker and dehydrate for a couple more hours.

Tropical Fruit Bars

Enjoy experimenting! Here's a sample idea:

1. Soak a bowl full of dehydrated mangoes, pears, and/or dehydrated apricots in water for an hour. Also soak a bowl of dates.
2. Soak a bowl of walnuts and almonds in water for at least 24 hours to help sprout the nuts.
3. In a food processor, blend the softened fruit with the nuts until mixed well and chopped up very small.
4. For variety, add a little vanilla flavoring, coconut, sesame seeds, cocoa powder.
5. For sweeter bars, add a little coconut syrup/honey/maple syrup or agave nectar. Usually the dates alone make it plenty sweet, but sometimes a little boost of sweetness is nice.
6. Finally, add a pinch of salt.
7. Spread the mixture onto the Teflon sheets and dehydrate for a few hours.
8. Flip the mixture and dehydrate for a few more hours.
9. Cut into long strips and roll it up like a fruit roll up.
10. Store in Ziplock bags.

Dinner

We like one pot dinners so if we have things like rice, we often make it at home and mix it in with the meal and dehydrate it all together. Makes for light weight packing as we only bring one pot!

Trail Yummy Bowls

An easy meal with many possibilities. Tastes great on the trail.

At home, make the Yummy Sauce:
½ c oil
½ c almonds
⅓ c nutritional yeast (or Brewer's yeast)
⅓ c garbanzo beans - drained
½ c silken tofu
½ c water
½ c lemon juice
2 garlic cloves
½ tsp salt
1 tsp curry powder

1. Blend nuts, beans, and oil in food processor. Add yeast and liquids one at a time. Puree until smooth.
2. Make rice. Add to rice a variety of items as you like: tomatoes, avocados, corn, salsa, black beans, cannellini beans, garbanzo beans. Add the sauce to your pot at the consistency that you like.

3. Spread the rice bowl/veggie/sauce mixture on dehydrator sheets. For our family of four, we put 11 cups of the mixture on the dehydrator.

4. Dehydrate for 7 to 10 hours until crispy. Store in a Ziplock bag.

On the trail:

1. Add enough water to the yummy bowl mixture to make the dehydrated meal and water equal the measurement written on your bag. Boil. Stir periodically. Turn stove off and leave covered for 20 minutes.

2. Turn oven back on and heat it again until hot, stirring occasionally. Serve and enjoy!

Minestrone Soup (Serves 6 to 8)
A tried and true hearty, veggie packed satisfying meal.

2 tbsp olive oil
2 c chopped onion
5 medium cloves garlic, minced
1½ to 2 tsp salt
1 stalk celery, minced
1 medium carrot, diced
1 small zucchini, diced
1 tsp oregano or 2 tsp of fresh rosemary
fresh black pepper, to taste
1 tsp basil
1 medium bell pepper, diced
3 to 4 cups (or more) water

1-14 ½ oz. can tomato puree (approx. 2 c)

1 to 1½ c cooked chickpeas, kidney beans, or cannellini beans

½ to 1 c dry pasta (we use a gluten free pasta)

1 or 2 medium sized ripe tomatoes, diced

½ c freshly minced parsley

Parmesan cheese

1. Heat the olive oil in a dutch oven. Add onion, garlic, and 1½ tsp salt. Saute over medium heat for about 5 minutes, then add celery, carrot, oregano, black pepper, and basil. Cover and cook over very low heat about 10 more minutes, stirring occasionally.

2. Add bell pepper, zucchini, water, and tomato puree. Cover and simmer about 15 minutes. Add beans and simmer another 5 minutes.

3. Bring the soup to a gentle boil. Add pasta, stir, and cook until the pasta is tender. Stir in the diced fresh tomatoes, and serve right away, topped with parsley and Parmesan.

4. For four people, scoop out 11 cups of the soup onto the Teflon sheets of the dehydrator and dehydrate for 7 to 8 hours. Flip the partially dried soup over and dehydrate a few more hours.

5. Store in Ziplock bag.

Split Pea Soup (Serves 8)

Comfort food on the trail. While this might be more of a winter meal, it settles well and tastes great on the cold nights at altitude that summer hiking can bring. Amazingly, it's one of our kids' favorite meals on the trail.

1 pound of split peas
1 ham bone or 2 ham hocks (with meat left on)
1 carrot, diced
1 onion, diced
1 stalk celery, diced
1 quarts water
1 tsp salt
¼ tsp pepper

1. Combine ingredients in slow-cooking pot. Cover and cook on low for 8-10 hours. Remove ham bone; cut meat off, dice, and return meat to soup.

2. Spread 11 cups onto Teflon lined dehydrator trays and dehydrate for 6 to 8 hours. Make sure you always are exact about how many cups of the meal you are putting on the trays.

3. At the trail, fill the pot with the dehydrated soup and then fill with water so that the combination equals the original amount you dehydrated. Boil. Turn stove off and let sit for at least 30 minutes. Turn the stove back on to heat it to your liking and serve.

4. Tastes great with tortillas.

Pesto Chicken Pasta

Anything with pesto tastes great to me. This is freshness on the trail. Hard to beat!

3 cans white chicken meat, dehydrated and packaged in a Ziplock bag

¾ c pesto sauce, *not* dehydrated, in a Ziplock bag. Double bag this to prevent leaking.

½ cup extra Parmesan cheese in a bag

bowtie pasta in a Ziplock bag that makes approximately 5 cups of cooked pasta

1. Put the assortment of bags in a gallon Ziplock bag and label.

2. At camp, put chicken in pot and fill the pot with water until it's about 1 inch higher than the chicken. Bring to a boil, then let it sit for an hour covered. Throw pasta and pesto sauce in the water and add more more water and boil.

3. When noodles are ready, stir well and serve with Parmesan cheese.

Camp Spaghetti (Serves 4 to 6)
This rehydrates so well and tastes just like it does at home. Got a rating of a 10 from our family. Cheers were loud during spaghetti feeds on the trail.

a bit of salsa
1 lb ground beef
½ onion
2 cloves garlic
24-36 oz of favorite pasta sauce
angel hair spaghetti or noodles to fill out approx 10 cups

1. Saute ground beef separately and the rinse the fat off in a colander.
2. Saute chopped onions, salsa, and garlic until well cooked. Add a jar of spaghetti sauce. You can add the beef that is rinsed back in right before putting it on the dehydrator trays.
3. Dehydrate in the dehydrator. Store in a Ziplock bag.
4. Pack spaghetti in another Ziplock bag. Put both bags in a gallon bag so the meal stays together. Can include a smaller Ziplock bag of Parmesan cheese.

On the trail:
1. Dump it all in the pot and fill until you reach 11 cups of volume.
2. Boil and then turn off. Stir, cover, and let sit for 45 minutes.
3. Turn stove on to heat it to desired temperature and then serve.

Middle Eastern Curry Vegetables and Rice

Delicious and easy. Goes great with mango chutney over over brown Basmati rice.

2 tbsp oil
1 c chopped onion
1 tbsp curry powder
1 tsp coriander
½ tsp coriander
½ tsp cumin
1½ c sliced carrots
½ medium head cauliflower, cut into small pieces for dehydrating
1 c red lentils, rinsed and drained
2½ c water
1 tsp sea salt or to taste
1 cup of rice

1. Heat the oil in a large, heavy kettle. Add the onion, curry powder, coriander, and cumin. Saute over medium heat until the onion begins to become translucent.
2. Add the carrots and the cauliflower, and stir for a few seconds. Then add the lentils and the water. Mix well. Raise the heat and bring the mixture to a boil. Lower the heat, stir, and cover. Simmer for about 40 minutes, stirring occasionally, until the lentils have formed a thick puree. Add the salt and mix well.
3. Make rice.
4. Mix rice into the curry.

5. Chop all veggies small enough for dehydrating and spread mixture onto Teflon sheets - ¼ inch thick at the most. For a family of four, we need 10 cups. Dehydrate for 6 to 8 hours, flip the mixture and dehydrate for a couple more hours.

6. Put mixture into ziploc bags.

On the trail:

1. Dump it all in the pot and fill until you reach 10 cups of volume.

2. Boil and then turn off. Stir, cover, and let sit for 20 to 25 minutes.

3. Turn stove on to heat it to desired temperature and then serve.

Summer Day Pasta (Serves 3 to 4)
Easy and so colorful, making for a fresh and delightful trail meal.

8 oz rice or corn pasta: shells or spirals
1 tbsp oil
1 c chopped onion
⅓ c sunflower seeds
3 medium carrots, shredded for easy dehydrating
1 tsp basil
2 tbsp tamari
2 tbsp nutritional yeast
1 tbsp balsamic vinegar
1 clove garlic, pressed

1 ripe tomato, chopped
½ c finely chopped parsley

1. Bring a large kettle of water to boil for cooking the pasta.
2. Meanwhile, heat the oil in a skillet. Add the onion and sunflower seeds. Saute until the onion begins to become tender. Add the carrots and the basil and saute until the carrots are tender (about 5 more minutes).
3. Cook the pasta al dente.
4. While the pasta cooks, mix together the tamari, yeast, vinegar, and garlic in a small bowl. Pour this mixture over the sauteed vegetables in the skillet. Add the tomato and the parsley. Mix well and heat, but do not simmer.
5. When the pasta is done, drain it and it to the vegetable mixture in the skillet.
6. Spread it on the Teflon sheets, ¼ inch thick and dehydrate for 6 to 8 hours.

On the trail:
1. Dump it all in the pot and fill until you reach 10 cups of volume.
2. Boil and then turn off.
3. Stir, cover, and let sit for 20 to 25 minutes.
4. Turn stove on to heat it to desired temperature and then serve.

Additional Resources

March, Laurie Ann. *A Fork in the Trail*
McHugh, Gretchen. *The Hungry Hiker's Book of Good Cooking*

1 Muir, John. *A Thousand-Mile Walk to the Gulf*. Ch. 4, (1916), p. 41-42.

2 Louv, Richard. *Last Child In The Woods*.

3 www.outdoorfoundation.org/pdf/ResearchParticipation2012 .pdf

4 www.outdoorfoundation.org/pdf/ResearchParticipation2012 .pdf

5 Tsunetsugu Y, Miyazaki Y. Measurement of absolute hemoglobin concentrations of prefrontal region by near-infrared time-resolved spectroscopy: examples of experiments and prospects. *J Physiol Anthropol Appl Human Sci.* 2005;24:469–472. doi: 10.2114/jpa.24.469.

6 Park, BJ, Y Tsunetsugu, T Kasetani, T Kagawa, Y Miyazaki. The physiological effects of shinrin-yoku (taking in the forest atmosphere or forest bathing): evidence from field experiments in 24 forests across Japan. *Environ Health Prev Med.* 2010;15:18–26. doi: 10.1007/s12199-009-0086-9.

7 Tsunetsugu, Y, Y Miyazaki, BJ Park. Trends in research related to "Shinrin-yoku" (taking in the forest atmosphere or forest bathing) in Japan. *Environ Health Prev Med.* 2010;15:27–37. doi: 10.1007/s12199-009-0091-z.

8 Li Q. Kawada. Effect of forest environments on human natural killer (NK) activity. *Int J Immunopathol Pharmacol.* 2011;24(1 Suppl):39S–44S.

9 Muir, John. *The Story of My Boyhood and Youth.* 1913, Ch. 6.

10 Muir, John. *The Yosemite.* 1912, p. 256.

11   www.webmd.com/epilepsy/guide/your-changing-hormones

12 Muir, John. *The Story of My Boyhood and Youth.* 1913, Ch. 6.

13 Muir, John. *My First Summer in the Sierra.* 1911, Ch. 6, journal entry July 27, 1868.

14 Clay, Rebecca A. "Green is Good for You," *Monitor on Psychology.* April 2001, Vol 32, No. 4, p 40.

15 www.apa.org/monitor/apr01/greengood.aspx.

16 Olshansky SJ, Douglas JP, Hershow RC, Layden J, Carnes BA, Brody J, et al. "A potential decline in life expectancy in the United States in the 21st century." *New England Journal of Medicine,* 2005;352:1138-45.

17 Cleland V, LA Baur, D Crawford, C Hume, J Salmon, A Timperio,. "A prospective examination of children's time spent outdoors, objectively measure physical activity and overweight." *International Journal of Obesity,* 2008;32:1685-93.

18 www.emory.edu/EMORY_REPORT/erarchive/2001/April.9/4_9_01frumkin.html

19 Muir, John. *The Mountains of California.* 1894, Ch. 7-8.

20 Montgomery, Lucy Maud. *Anne of Green Gables.* 1908.

21 Muir, John. *Our National Parks.* 1901, p. 56.

22 Muir, John. *My First Summer in the Sierra.* 1911, p. 231.

23 Muir, John. "American Forests," *Atlantic Monthly,* No. 80, August, 1897.

24 Muir, John. *Our National Parks.* 1901, Ch. 10.

25 Young, Samuel Hall. *Alaska Days with John Muir.* 1915, Ch. 7.

26 www.apa.org/monitor/apr01/greengood.aspx

27 www.news.cornell.edu/releases/april03/nature.kid.stress.ssl.html

28 Kellert, Stephen R. *Building for Life: Designing and Understanding the Human-Nature Connection.*

29 Louv, Richard. *Last Child In The Woods.*

30 Pyle, Robert Michael. *The thunder tree: Lessons from an urban wildland.* Boston: Houghton Mifflin, 1993.

31 Reed, Edward. *The Necessity of Experience.* Yale University Press. 1996.

32 http://scienceline.org/2010/08/can-a-stroll-in-the-park-replace-the-psychiatrist's-couch/

33 www.apa.org/monitor/apr01/greengood.aspx

34 http://lhhl.illinois.edu/adhd.htm

35 Delate, Thomas, Ph.D., Alan J. Gelenberg, MD, Brenda R. Motheral, PhD, Valarie A. Simmons, MS. "Trends in the Use of Antidepressants in a National Sample of Commercially Insured Pediatric Patients 1998 to 2002." *Psychiatric Services* 2004; doi: 10.1176/appi.ps.55.4.387

36 Kahn Jr, Peter H., and Stephen R. Kellert. *Children and nature: Psychological, sociocultural, and evolutionary*

investigations. Peter H Kahn Jr & Stephen R Kellert. MIT Press, 2002.

37 Muir, John. *The Mountains of California.* 1894, Ch. 8

38 www.webmd.com/a-to-z-guides/altitude-sickness-references#abk7532

39 www.sce.com/PowerandEnvironment/PowerGeneration/Big CreekHydro/default.htm

40 www.sce.com/PowerandEnvironment/PowerGeneration/Big CreekHydro/Relicensing/documentation.htm#factsheets

41 Muir, John. *Our National Parks.* 1901, Ch. 1.

42 Muir, John. *Our National Parks.* 1901, Ch. 1.

43 Muir, John. *My First Summer in the Sierra.* 1911, Ch. 6, journal entry July 26, 1869.

44 Louv, Richard. *Last Child In The Woods.*

45 http://www.ahaparenting.com/parenting-tools/raise-great-kids/intellegent-creative-child/boredom-busters-good-for-kids.

46 http://www.mudpiemamas.com/2013/07/21/the-beauty-of-boredom/

47 "Media Use by Children Younger Than 2 Years," *Pediatrics.* Volume 128, Number 5, November 2011.

48 http://www.kff.org/entmedia/mh012010pkg.cfm. Generation M2: Media in the lives of 8 to 18 year olds.

49 Kubey, Robert. "Television Dependence, Diagnosis, and Prevention." Associate Professor, Department of Journalism & Media Studies. Rutgers University, New Brunswick, NJ. 1996.

50 McIlwraith, R. D. (1990). "Theories of television addiction." Talk to the American Psychological Association, Boston, MA, August.

51 Klesges, RC, LM Klesges, ML Shelton. "Effects of television on metabolic rate: potential implications for childhood obesity," *Pediatrics*. 1993 Feb; 91(2):281-6.

52 John Muir, Letter to Jeanne C. Carr, Undated, estimated as September, 1874

53 Moore, R. "The need for nature: A childhood right," *Social Justice*. 1997. 24(3):203-220.

54 *Ibid*.

55 Muir, John. *The Yosemite* (1912), p. 256.

56 http://www.bostern.com/blog/2010/10/16/16462/

57 Muir, John. *My First Summer in The Sierra*. 1911, Ch. 5, journal entry July 20, 1869.

58 *Ibid*.

59 Muir, John. *My First Summer in The Sierra*. 1911, Ch. 2, journal entry June 23, 1869.

60 Wolfe, Linnie Marsh, editor. *John of the Mountains: The Unpublished Journals of John Muir*. University of Wisconsin Press, 1938, republished 1979.

61 *The Pylet*. Pyles Boys Camp newsletter, August 1997.

62 Louv, p. 37.

63 Louv, p. 67.

64 Muir, John. *John of the Mountains: The Unpublished Journals of John Muir*. 1938, p. 208.

65 "John Muir's Menu," *Sierra*. (Vol. 79, Issue 6), p. 66, Nov-Dec, 1994.

66 Karr, Kris. *Crazy, Sexy, Diet*. p. 3

67 "Preventing Chronic Diseases: a Vital Investment": Geneva, World Health Organization, 2005.

68 2008-2013 Action Plan for the Global Strategy for the Prevention and Control of Noncommunicable Diseases: Geneva, World Health Organization, 2008.

69 Letter to Jeanne C. Carr, written near Snelling in Merced Co., CA, July 26, 1868 in *John Muir: Letters to a Friend.* (Boston and New York: Houghton Mifflin Company, 1915).

70 Letter to Jeanne C. Carr, written near Snelling in Merced Co., CA, July 26, 1868 in *John Muir: Letters to a Friend.* (Boston and New York: Houghton Mifflin Company, 1915).

71 Baughman, Michael. *A River Seen Right.* Lyons Press, 1995.

72 Muir, John. *My First Summer in the Sierra.* 1911, Ch. 8, journal entry August 14, 1869.

73 Muir, John. *My First Summer in the Sierra.* 1911, Ch. 6, journal entry July 27, 1868.

74 Muir, John. *Our National Parks.* 1901, Ch. 2.

75 Powell, Lawrence Clark. "John Muir: The Mountains of California," *The Creative Literature of the Golden State: Essays on the Books and Their Writers.* Santa Barbara, Capra Press, 1971.

76 Muir, John. *The Mountains of California.* Ch. 10.

77 Palmer, Albert Wentworth, 1879. Boston, New York [etc.]: The Pilgrim press.

78 John Muir, *Our National Parks.* 1901, Ch. 3.

79 Smith, Alexander McCall. *The No. 1 Detective Agency, Book 1.* Anchor Pub. 2003.

80 Muir, John. *My First Summer in the Sierra.* 1911, Ch. 2.

First, I could never have accomplished the monumental mountain of a task of getting my ideas in written form and sticking with it until publication without the undying encouragement and support of my best friend, lifetime hiking partner, and husband of 20 years, Cory. I love our dance. Thank you for patiently going our pace all these years and giving up your 500 mile hiking summers to indoctrinate all three of us into your passion for the mountains. You could have just left every summer for your annual trek, but instead, you have taken the time to teach us, secure our gear, and plan family-friendly trips even when you were longing for more adventure, longer miles, and higher peaks.

I also want to take this time to give a shout out to our two kids, Cade - our courageous first born and Bekah - our "all-in" second born.

Cade: You have set the pace for our family - both literally (it's hard to keep up with you on the trail!) and figuratively. You have always just been willing to go for it and give it your best effort from the time you could first walk until now when we have to ask you to wait for us at the turns in the path. You've set the attitude example of not complaining and hiking with a cheerful spirit so that when your younger sister looked up to you, she just fell in line with that mindset. You have found your own unique ways to intersect with the wilderness through fly-fishing and have persevered through the disappointments of not catching a thing to now routinely catching 20 to 60 Trout in an evening. It's a testament to your perseverance and determination to never give up.

Bekah: We seem to set the summer's goals without even worrying that you are smaller, shorter, and younger because whether it's a 5 mile day or an 18 mile day, you are eager and soaking up every second of the time out there. You cry because the hike is over, not because it lays ahead. You are so content and at home on the trail it amazes me and inspires me. You are only 12 years old but those little legs of yours have walked over 1000 miles in the last 5 summers. I love the way you cheer your brother on along the shores of the lakes, being the first to unhook his catch and throw it back in the lake. You sit by my side and journal while I journal (writing your own best-seller) and you accompany daddy on his photo shoots in the evenings. You just love everything about being with the family in the mountains and it shows in your ever present smile, giggles, and continuous song that you sing throughout the days.

Thank you to my editor, Jami Carpenter of Red Pen Girl (http://www.redpengirl.com/) who took my rough-around-the-edges manuscript and made it pop and sing with style.

Thank you to my critique group friends Amanda Curley and Danielle Harris. We unloaded a lot of red ink on each other's work, asked the tough questions, and didn't let each other give up.

Thanks to my amazing graphic designer Micah Chrzan who created a cover that captures the awe of the mountains and draws you in to turn to the first page of the book and maybe to even put the book down and get outside!

Many thanks to my mother-in-law and father-in-law, Marsha and Leonard, who helped shuttle us from trailhead to trailhead, cheering us on as we tackled our first through-hike, and for periodically asking me how the book was coming along so that I wouldn't quit before the finish line.

And finally, thank you to my parents, Charles and Diane, who always believed in me and would lovingly welcome and accept me whether I hiked 1000 miles and made it to the top of Whitney or not. That's the kind of love that births kids that think they can not only climb mountains, but move them too.

About the Author

Julie O'Neill has an undergraduate degree in exercise and sports science, marketing and Spanish and a master's degree in health, English as a second language, and Spanish education. She's a full time teacher with a passion for healthy, active lifestyles for both adults and children. She has been published in Guideposts magazine as well as placed as a top-finalist in a national Guideposts writing competition. As well, she has spoken at numerous events and venues including REI.

Julie lives in the Pacific Northwest with her husband and two children. She has been backpacking for nearly twenty years. Off the trail, Julie enjoys running, yoga, and is often found curled up with tea, reading a good book.

Living Without Walls is her first book.

Follow Julie on Facebook:

www.facebook.com/authorJulieONeill/

Check out her blog, where no adventure is too big or too small:

julieaoneill.wordpress.com

⇀⁓↽

Made in the USA
Lexington, KY
10 June 2017